Library of Congress Cataloging-in-Publication Data

Gould, Roberta, 1946-
Making cool crafts & awesome art: a kids' treasure trove of fabulous fun / by Roberta Gould.
p. cm.
"Williamson kids can! book."
Summary: Explains a variety of hands-on art and craft activities, incorporating storytelling, ethnic cooking, music, nature, cultural games, and more.
ISBN 1-885593-11-2
1. Handicraft—Juvenile literature. [1. Handicraft.] I. Title.
TT160.G68 1997
745.5—dc21   96-51658
CIP
AC

Credits
Cover design: Joseph Lee Design, Inc.
Interior design: Joseph Lee Design, Inc.
Photographs: Roberta Gould
Printing: Capital City Press

Williamson Publishing Co.
P.O. Box 185
Charlotte, VT 05445
1-800-234-8791

Manufactured in the United States of America

10 9 8 7 6 5 4 3 2

Notice: The information contained in this book is true, complete, and accurate to the best of our knowledge. All recommendations and suggestions are made without any guarantees on the part of the author or Williamson Publishing. The author and publisher disclaim all liability incurred in connection with the use of this information.

A Williamson *Kids Can!* ® Book

MAKING COOL CRAFTS & AWESOME ART

A Kids' Treasure Trove of Fabulous Fun

Roberta Gould

Photographs by Roberta Gould

WILLIAMSON PUBLISHING COMPANY

CHARLOTTE, VERMONT

For Stanley Robert Gould, 1919–1996, who had a very interesting life because he didn't understand the meaning of the word bored.

Acknowledgements

I want to thank:

My husband for being so loving;

My kids for being a lot of fun;

My parents for allowing me the freedom to be adventurous;

My sister for being continuously supportive;

My brother and his wife for their honest encouragement;

Jane Demmert (in Juneau) for knowing I would be good at learning from the old
    people and teaching to the young;

Loren Kramer for sharing his wonderful Kentucky holler with me;

Arminda Stacy of Lick Branch, Kentucky, for letting me learn to milk on her cow;

Antioch College for showing me what real education is;

Elaine Schooley, dancer, for allowing wildness and authenticity to emerge;

Julie Winkelstein for being full of ideas and willing to try almost anything;

Fellow writers Raphael Shevelev, Mani Feniger, Ernest Callenbach, and Naomi Lucks
    for holding my hand when I needed it.

Thanks to these wonderful (and photogenic) kids for their crucial contribution to the book:

Eileen Beil, Karen Nakasato, Kimberly MeiAller, Sarah Dobjensky, Sophie Winik,

Zoe Griffith, Zach Walters, Yoshi Smith, Waylon James Bacon, Walker Shapiro, Vivienne S. Carlsen, Vanessa Wellbery, Tess, Tara Mongkolpuet, Summer Jackson, Stefan Goldberg, Sophia Perkis, Sierra Liebman (C.C.L.), Sherry Lee Aragon, Sarah Streit, Sarah Rose Barrett, Sarah Leff, Sara Schultz, Ryan Mueller, Romana Ferretti, Richard Michel, Rebecca Krow-Boniske, Rae Ann Winkelstein-Duveneck, Rachel Shoshana Berman, Peter Rudiak-Gould, Osiris Henderson, Nicole Berger, Nicholas Danby, Nathaniel Rudiak-Gould, Nathan Rynerson, Nariman Safizadeh, Molly Munch Di Grazia, Molly Gould, Miya Kitahara, Miya Frank, Mitchell Green, Michi, Michelle Kim, Michael Clement, Meir Berman, Maya Sanchez-Haller, Max Green, Marta Blanchard, Marjorie Rose Gomez, Marcus Toriumi, Lyal Michel, Lucia Graves, Leif Pipersky, Lauren Finzer, Kyle Kemp, Kory Sutherland, Kiri Jones, Katie Jensen, Katherine Winkelstein-Duveneck, Karl Robinson, Kari Gjerde, Kaitlin Friedman, Joy Proctor, Jonathan Ball, Joe Holden-Stern, Jed Loveday-Brown, Jacob Winik, Ilana Caplan, Honey Bee Evans, Hester Chambers Mills, Hannah K. Moore, Francesca Danby, Fiona Gladstone, Emma Silvers, Emily Zubritsky, Emily Walters, Elizabeth, Daveed Daniele Diggs, Darleen Ashlee Aragon, Daniel Reichman, Daniel Lawrence, Cor Despota, Colleen Smallfield, Clare Nicole Kruger, Casey Jackson, Carrie Peterson, Carrie Meldgin, Caroline Thow, Carmen Ruda, Carlos I. Sempere C., Carl Gould, Caitlin, Brigette Stump-Vernon, Bill Holden-Stern, Bianca Smith, Bethany Lynn Woolman, Ben Rudiak-Gould, B. B. Said, Asa Kalama, A(o)sa Jonmarker, Arwen Thoman, Anya Goldstein, Amber Marion Bacon, Allison Menzimer, Acacia Quien, Ben Kalama, Anya Black, and anon.

MAKING COOL CRAFTS & AWESOME ART

TABLE

CONTENTS

MAKING COOL CRAFTS & AWESOME ART

Welcome, Welcome, Every Guest

ROUND

A minor
2-4 parts
Circa 1800s

FUN TIMES AHEAD

Making Cool Crafts & Awesome Art is loaded with so much to do, you'll have trouble figuring out where to start — so just dive in anywhere!

You'll find you can make most of the crafts without any help. That's because in art there really is no "right" way to do something.

Relax and let your creative mind go to work. For instance, don't worry about not having the exact tool or the precise kind of paint for a given project. Use whatever you have on hand that you think will work. Improvising adds spice to life, and who knows — maybe you'll figure out a better way! Many of the crafts use materials that are found around your home, yard, or school. And best of all, most of the materials are free.

Invite your friends to do these crafts with you, or make them on your own. Along the way, you'll learn to throw away less and create more, to take things that aren't being used for their original purpose and find new uses for them — to make something magical from something mundane!

ROUND
Shalom Chaverim
ROUND

(Farewell Good Friends)
E minor
2 parts
Traditional Hebrew

Sha - lom, cha-ver-im, sha - lom, cha-ver-im, sha - lom, sha - lom, la
Mi   La   La Ti Do   La   Do Do Re Mi Mi   La   So   Mi   Mi

hit   ra____ ot,   la   hit   ra____ ot, sha - lom,   sha-___ lom.   Sha
La   Mi Re Do   Re   Mi   Do Ti La Mi   La   Ti Do   La   Mi

Everything Unique

Look at the kids in this book; notice that everyone's project looks different. Don't try to make your crafts look like any others — yours will be special just because you made them, no matter what the outcome.

Feel free to change the projects, to cut them short, or to expand them. Use these ideas as a springboard for self-discovery. Each time you undertake a project, you'll undoubtedly come up with new ideas and slightly better ways of doing things! That's what creativity is all about — looking at existing methods and then building on them in ways that reflect you and your special interests. The special dimension to making art is YOU, so allow it to flourish.

Fun for All Ages

All craft projects are labeled by various levels of challenge, just to give you some idea of what's involved. But you are talented enough to do any of them! So don't let a more difficult rating keep you from any of these projects.

Level of challenge: 1

If you are a second grader or older, you should be able to make these projects fairly easily. Younger kids will want some help from grown-ups or siblings. A parent or teacher can also use these projects with a classroom-size group.

Level of challenge: 2

If you are in fourth grade, these projects will be fairly easy. Younger kids will benefit from help from friends and relatives. Grown-ups working with groups of kids should have a few helpers.

Level of challenge: 3

These projects are just a little bit harder and involved. Grown-ups working with groups of younger kids will need several parents or older kids to help.

Making Your Environment Fit You

Setting up a fun place for crafting is important. You'll need a place where you can spread out lots of materials, where you'll have plenty of space to be creative, and where you won't have to worry about cleaning up right after. In this environment, you can make amazing things!

Outdoors is the best place to work. Everyone likes being outside, especially after a day indoors. The air is fresher, ventilation isn't a problem, you can be noisy, there's plenty of space, and it's easier to clean up!

Saving for the Future

You can save all sorts of craft materials — from recycled plastic milk jugs to broken electronic items — to have on hand when you make art. Having shelves of various art materials is a good idea, and it's also fun to have boxes of goodies for specific projects. You could put all the pieces of broken electronic odds and ends and all the face-shaped and robot-shaped packaging into a box labeled ROBOT. Save the supplies until you have a nice stash; then do a project. When you set up a creative environment, you'll often be surprised and delighted with the amazing things you can make. It's especially fun to set out 5 or 10 random items. Examine them, turn them over, and before you know it — bingo! — a creative idea will spring to mind.

Wait! Don't Throw That Away

Your family may already be doing a great job of minimizing the amount of packaging brought into your home by "wise shopping," but you may still be throwing away a lot of wonderful craft materials without even knowing it. For instance, that empty roll from the plastic tape is precious — it's a wheel for a car or a game piece. Those empty film canisters could be used to make toy "binoculars" and the lids used to make doll's glasses. That empty dental floss container would make a small backpack for a claymation figure (see page 132), and the inside mechanism would work perfectly as a little wheel.

Do you have clothes with worn knees or elbows? Save the buttons for necklaces or doll's eyes. Or, dress a scarecrow in an old pair of outgrown jeans (see page 120). After you've used all the paper in your spiral binder, keep the metal spiral and twist it into a useful sculpture. Soon you'll begin to see that it's downright hard to find things you can't put to use in your craft projects!

Waste Not, Want Not

Here are some items to have around if you want to be able to make almost anything. Don't worry if you don't have all of these things — this is just your wish list!

Balloons, broken (keep out of reach of toddlers)
Beads (from rejected necklaces or garage sales)
Small bottles (from vanilla extract or spices)
Boxes — all sizes and thicknesses
Bubble wrap (from packaging and torn mailing envelopes)
Bread clasps and twist ties
Cloth (from old clothes, scraps from sewing)
Corks
Corn husks
Cotton balls (from pill bottles)
Deck of cards (incomplete)
Egg cartons
Envelopes (used)
Film containers and "goof" negatives
Foam (from rug pads)
Foil, aluminum
Hangers and tubes
Lace (from sewing projects)
Leather and fur (from worn car seat covers, slippers)
Magazines, old
Metal bottle caps and disks (from frozen juice)

Milk cartons
Miscellaneous metal (from broken items)
Netting (from packaging oranges, potatoes, and onions)
Packaging popcorn or pellets (from mailings)
Pantyhose (with runs)
Paper (one side printed)
Paper clips
Paper cups (from fast food restaurants)
Paper towel and bath tissue rolls
Pinecones (collected on walks)
Plastic bottles and jugs
Plastic containers and lids, all sizes
Plastic packaging
Popsicle sticks
Puzzle pieces (from incomplete puzzles)
Ribbon (from presents)
Ropes (miscellaneous)
Rubber bands (from newspapers)
Shells (only from very plentiful beaches)
Shoulder pads
Stamps (used)
Stiff paper, cards (from holidays, packaging)
Strawberry baskets
Straws (washed, used)
String (from wrapping, shoelaces, etc.)

Stuffing (from pillows)
Styrofoam™ and other trays (from fruits and veggies only)
Tapes (cassette, other; used, unneeded, taken apart)
Telephone wire (from telephone company)
Twigs, rocks, dried garden stuff
Wax (from cheese wrapping, old candle stubs)
Wood scraps (from free boxes at carpentry shops and lumberyards)
Wrapping paper (from birthdays, holidays)
Yarn

From the Store

These are things you may need to buy, but you'll find many uses for them.

Awl (see Safety First on page 12)
Chalk
Clay, modeling or homemade (see page 134)
Colored paper
Colored pens, markers, pencils
Crayons
Drill (small, cordless; see Safety First on page 12)

Food coloring
Glitter
Glue sticks
Glue, white craft
Hammer, nails (see Safety First)
Needles, thread
Paint: acrylic, fabric
Paintbrushes
Permanent pens (use outdoors or in well-ventilated room)

Pins, safety pins
Scissors (strong, metal ones)
Staplers
Steak knives, serrated
String
Tape: wide packaging, masking and clear
Toothpicks
Warm glue gun (see Glue Gun Safety on page 16)

Safety First

Some of the projects in this book require tools that can be dangerous when used incorrectly. Always have a grown-up supervise while working with knives, hammers, glue guns, awls, and kitchen appliances.

Anything Is Possible!

After making some of the projects in this book, you'll begin to look at everything with the question: "How can I use that?" Anything is possible!

Don't let yourself feel overwhelmed by all the activities in this book. Just do one! If you just think of the part you're working on right then, rather than thinking of the whole job, you'll do fine. You can do almost anything you want if you decide to. So just go for it!

As you get involved in making the exciting crafts ahead, you'll never know the meaning of the word *bored!* So fire up your imagination, let the creative spirit enter your heart, and get started expressing yourself. And always remember: There are no two of you and there won't be two crafts that look or function the same way. First and foremost, this book is about who you are!

GRASSES, VINES, & MORE

C raft projects that use grasses and vines are fun and inexpensive to make. You can make these beautiful things with natural and wild materials, and you'll feel good because you're doing your part to save the earth. Put a homemade wreath on your front door for all to enjoy. Revive the old European custom of going door to door in your neighborhood in the early morning on May Day (May 1) and putting baskets or wreaths of flowers at the doorsteps of your friends' and neighbors' homes.

ROUND · Aleluia · ROUND

Mozart
F major
2-3 parts
Circa 1700s

1
A - le-lu ia, A - le - lu - ia____, A - le-__ lu-__ ia, A - le-__ lu-__ ia.
So La La So Fa Mi Mi Mi Mi Fa Fa So La La So Fa Mi So Fa Mi Re Do

2
A - le-lu ia, A - le - lu - ia,____ A - le-__ lu-__ ia, A - le-__ lu-__ ia.
Mi Fa Fa Mi Re Do Do Do Di Re Re Mi Fa Fa Mi Re Do Mi Re Do Ti Do

3
A - le - lu - ia. A - le - lu -__ ia.
Do Do So So Ti Do La Fa So Do

1 hour gathering and pruning *(optional)*
24 hours soaking
2 hours creating

VINE BASKETS

*B*askets come from many lands and are vastly different in size and shape, largely because each culture weaves them from plants that are native — that is, growing in the region where they live. Baskets differ also in how they're used — from gathering vegetables and flowers from the garden to holding groceries instead of using brown bags. You'll be making your baskets out of vines and other flexible plants that you can find around your neighborhood.

WHAT YOU NEED

- Grapevines or other thin, flexible, strong vines
- Yarn
- Weaving material (flat, flexible strips), such as thin vines, yarn, or grass at least 15" (40 cm) long
- Cool-melt glue gun (see Glue Gun Safety on page 16) or white craft glue

WHAT YOU DO

Making the Framework

❶ Select 2 strong vines that are 4' to 6' (1.25 m to 2 m) long. If your vine isn't freshly pruned, you may need to soak it in water overnight to soften it.

❷ Make a wreath from each vine by forming a circle that is about 20" (50 cm) in circumference and then winding the rest of the vine's length in and out around the circle. (See page 28.) One wreath will become the rim of the basket and the other will be the handle and the bottom of the basket.

❸ Tie the 2 wreaths at right angles to hold them in place temporarily.

❹ To secure the 2 wreaths with a God's eye corner (see God's Eye Practice), tie a 1 to 2 yard (1 m to 2 m) piece of yarn at one of the crosses where the 2 wreaths meet. Make a strong God's eye, using all the yarn. Make sure the X is held securely in place by your yarn and tie the end of the yarn.

God's Eye Practice

Use a 3' (1 m) length of yarn to tie 2 Popsicle sticks in the center. Wind the yarn around the first Popsicle stick; then, over and around the next Popsicle stick; then, over and around the next one. Continue around and around until you run out of yarn.

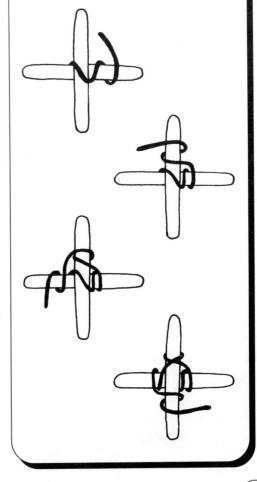

Handle

Rim

New spokes

Weaving

❶ Weave with the long strands of material to form the basket bottom. Starting at one rim, weave a strand in and out, in and out, from one rim to the other and back to the first rim.

❺ Cut 4 or 6 vines to about 10" (25 cm) lengths; then, curve them so they're caught in the God's eyes at each side of the basket. They will form spokes for the basket bottom. Remember that you should not put spokes between the rim and the handle, or you will end up with a woven sphere!

❻ Glue the spokes securely in the yarn.

Glue Gun Safety

Glue guns are wonderful tools, but always use caution when using them. Ask a grown-up to help you find a place to set up the glue gun to make sure you can use it safely. Be sure the electrical cord isn't in the way when using scissors, and avoid touching the tip end, which can be very hot.

2 When you use up one strand, start in with another.

3 Continue until the whole basket bottom is woven. Secure the ends of each strand.

People from many cultures gather the natural materials used in basket-making from the land. Look around your backyard or ask around the neighborhood for materials to make a basket. Do you have any grape- or other vines growing? Gather

Finding Nature's Bounty

some and see if they're flexible. Weeds that entwine themselves around trees also make good weaving material, because they are flexible — plus you are freeing up the tree. If you still come up short on natural materials, ask a local gardener to save vine prunings from the yards he or she works in. Buy your materials from a craft or florist shop only as a last resort.

Cooking in Baskets

The Native Californians didn't use the local clay for pottery; instead, they made watertight baskets to use for cooking. But how, you might ask, was water boiled or food cooked in a vine basket without the basket burning? The coastal Miwok solved the problem by heating rocks in the fire and then putting them in the water in the basket. They would stir constantly, cooking whatever was in the basket without ever burning it.

Overnight soaking, plus ¹/₂ hour
for each project

WHEAT SHAPES

For 9,000 years, wheat has been such an important food crop in Europe, Russia, the Middle East, and India that people give thanks with harvest rituals, some of which are still practiced today. Traditionally, people would gather some of the best or the last stalks of wheat from the harvest and make them into beautiful shapes. The harvesters would gather around and sing a beautiful chant to the spirit of the wheat, which could be heard for miles. In England, harvesters would then break into wonderful laughter and throw their caps in the air. You might want to try it!

The Power of Tradition

On the first day of winter (known as the solstice) in Denmark, Sweden, and Norway, people used to tie wheat sheaves to the top of a tall pole to ward away evil spirits that raced around on the cold dark nights of winter. They may have been inspired by the howling winds of winter storms. Nowadays, people continue the tradition because they are happy to feed the hungry winter birds.

WHAT YOU NEED

- 10 or more wheat or rye stalks with flowers, 12" (30 cm) long (look in craft stores), or tall, wild grasses
- Thin wire or red yarn cut to 3" (7.5 cm) lengths, at least 10
- Red ribbons

Wheat Wreaths

WHAT YOU DO

1 Soak the wheat or rye in luke-warm water overnight; then, tie 3 wheat or wild grass stalks securely at the head (flower) end with wire.

2 Braid the 3 stalks by putting the right stalk over the middle stalk; then, the left over the middle; then, the right over the middle; and the left over the middle, until you braid to the bottom. (See page 54 for braiding tips.)

3 Curve the braid around in a circle and tie it in place with the wire.

4 To cover the wire, tie a ribbon in a bow.

5 Make a hook out of wire or use an ornament hook to hang the wreath.

Let It Grow!

Too bad most people mow their lawns. If you let lawn grass grow, it gets tall and beautiful and has pretty grass flowers. It's hard to notice there's more than one kind of grass when it's cut close to the ground, but if you let it grow and go to seed, you'll see how some grasses have lacy, compact flowers, and others have prickly seeds. Start a wild spot at the edge of your lawn or throw some wheat or rye seeds out in an unclaimed patch of land and grow your own stalks.

Scandinavian Hearts

1 Tie 6 wheat or wild grass stalks securely at the head (flower) end with wire.

2 Tie the stalks with wire again, about 2" (5 cm) down from the heads.

3 Divide the 6 stalks into 2 groups of 3 and braid each group of 3 in a tight braid so you have 2 braids. Secure the ends of each braid with wire.

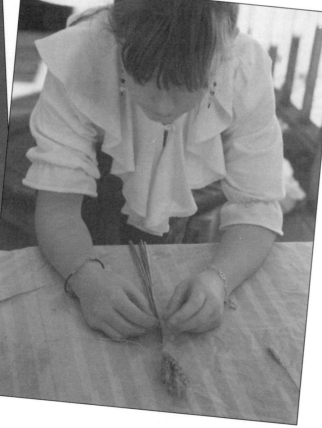

MAKING COOL CRAFTS & AWESOME ART

6 Attach a wire or an ornament hook and hang the heart as a decoration or give it as a gift.

4 Curve the braids around to form 2 halves of a heart; then attach them with wire behind the first tie.

5 Tie a ribbon in a bow to cover the wire.

Special Braids

Use 4 stalks for the wreath and 8 stalks for the heart for a beautiful, but more challenging, braid. Spread out the 4 stalks as spokes of a wheel, leaving space for an imaginary fifth stalk. Fold #2 to the empty space and fold #4 to the new space where #2 was. Then, fold #1 to the new space and fold #3 to the space where #1 was. Repeat until the stalks are used up. Secure the ends of the braid with wire.

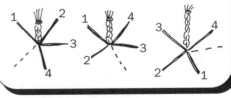

Star of David

To make this traditional Jewish shape, you first need to cut the flower heads off the wheat or wild grass stalks. Or, pull apart an old beach mat (ask a grown-up first) and use the individual stalks for your stars. The Star of David has 6 points formed by 2 overlapping triangular shapes.

❶ Tie a bundle of twelve 10" (25 cm) stalks securely in the middle with wire.

❷ Bunch the stalks into 6 groups of 4 and tie securely, about 2" (5 cm) from the center, forming the spokes of a wheel.

❸ Join 2 ends from one spoke with 2 ends from the next closest spoke, and tie them about 1/2" (1 cm) from the ends.

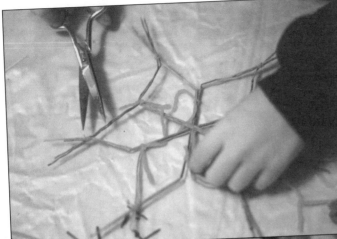

Wheat Figure or Angel

1 Cut 6 to 12 stalks to twice as long as you want your figure to be; then, tie the bundle in the center with wire.

2 Fold the stalks in half and tie them where you want the neck to be.

3 Cut 6 to 8 stalks for arms or wings. Lift up half the stalks to the neck and put the arms in between the front and back stalks. Tie the main bunch where you want the waist to be.

4 Trim the arms or wings to the desired shape and length; then, attach a hook and hang.

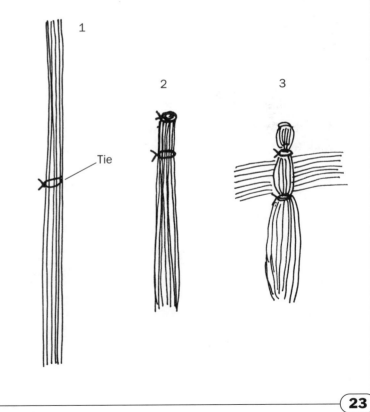

4 Continue around the circle until all the spokes are tied.

5 Add a wire hanger and hang your star in the window or on the wall.

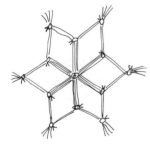

Straw Goat

*I*n Finland and Norway, straw long-horned goats are made to go under the Christmas tree, a throwback to an earlier tradition where the goat was the pet of the Norse god Thor. At Christmastime, Scandinavian children still like to dress up as a goat and be playful.

1 Cut 20 to 30 stalks about 8" (20 cm) long and tie the bunch with red yarn at 4" (10 cm) and 6" (15 cm) from one end for the goat's hind quarters.

2 Bend down 6 stalks for each rear leg and tie with red yarn.

3 Braid the top 3 stalks into a tail and tie. Then, carefully cut off the rest of the stalks at the rear end.

4 At the front end, bend down 6 stalks for each leg.

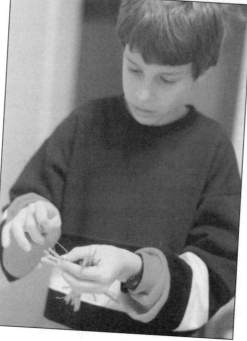

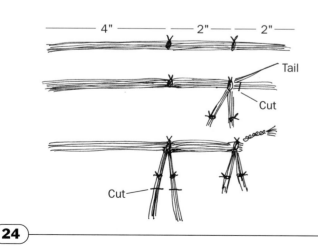

5 Trim 2" (5 cm) off the front legs and tie. Then, slowly bend the remaining stalks up to form the neck, being careful not to break them. Tie at the head.

6 Braid 2 horns out of 6 stalks (3 stalks for each horn).

7 Carefully bend down and tie the rest of the stalks to make the face.

WREATHS

I t's traditional to make circular wreaths at the time of the winter solstice (December 22) to represent the way the seasons go around and around forever. The wreaths are made of plants to symbolize the ability of the earth to produce life.

Solstice Celebrations

The winter solstice (December 22) is the shortest day of the year, and even though the weather gets colder after that date, most people are glad to see the hours of sun increase again and are hopeful that spring is a few months away.

2 hours

Nature's Wreaths

M*ake beautiful wreaths from "found" objects in your own backyard or a favorite park.*

WHAT YOU DO

❶ Trace around the larger plate onto the cardboard. Cut out the circle.

❷ Trace and cut out the smaller plate in the center of the larger cardboard circle. (If the cardboard is thick, you may need grown-up help.)

WHAT YOU NEED

• Thick cardboard from boxes
• 5" and 10" (12.5 cm and 25 cm) plates or other flat, circular objects for tracing
• Nature's found objects (interesting branches, seeds, nuts, pebbles, pinecones)
• Scissors or serrated knife (see Knife Safety)
• White craft glue or cool-melt glue gun (see Glue Gun Safety on page 16)

Knife Safety

Serrated steak knives are useful tools, but always be sure you work on a flat, steady surface when cutting, and never work with knives without a grown-up around. Serrated knives work like saws for cutting through harder materials, and their pointed ends are good for piercing cardboard and plastic.

Natural Candle Holders

Make a small circular or oval base of heavy cardboard or wood. You might want to ask a grown-up to cut a round slice of a large branch. Glue on a candle and some of the beautiful wild things you've collected and use as a center-piece for your dinner table.

3 Glue the found objects you gathered on the plain brown side of the cardboard. Try to cover the whole surface of the cardboard.

4 Let the wreath dry completely; then, hang it on your door.

1 hour pruning
24 hours soaking
2 to 3 hours assembly

Vine Wreaths

*T*he Romans gave wreaths as gifts for the
*New Year because gifts were supposed to
bring good luck — an old tradition that's fun
to continue with your family.*

WHAT YOU NEED

- Grapevines or other vines
- Green garbage bag twist ties
- Pruning shears

WHAT YOU DO

1 Use freshly pruned vines or
soak dry vines in water for 24
hours in a large tub, bathtub,
or clean garbage can.

2 Starting with the larger end
of the vine, form a circle 16" to
18" (40 cm to 45 cm) around
and tie it securely with a green
twist tie.

3 Wind the rest of the vine in
and out around the circle until
it's used up.

4 Add another vine and begin
where the first vine ended,
winding in and out around the
circle.

5 Continue until you have gone around at least 4 times, but no more than 10 times. (With very thin vines you may need to go around as many as 20 times for a strong wreath.)

6 Let the wreath dry for about an hour; then, decorate (see Decorating Techniques on page 30).

Rest on Your Laurels

Early wreaths were worn on the head to symbolize great achievements. In ancient Greece, wreaths made of laurel leaves were awarded for excellence in athletics and music. In ancient Rome, laurel wreaths were awarded as prizes for military achievements. Make a wreath to crown yourself. What trait or achievement are you most proud of?

1 hour pruning
1 to 2 hours assembly

Coat Hanger Wreaths

WHAT YOU NEED

- All-metal coat hanger
- Evergreen boughs
- Vegetable-wrapping wires (lettuce, spinach), paper removed
- Green garbage bag twist ties

WHAT YOU DO

❶ Bend the coat hanger into a circle. Leave the hook in place to hang the wreath later.

❷ Tie green boughs to the circle, using wire to secure them in several places. Add boughs until the wreath is thick and the wire is completely covered.

Gift wreath. Consider unusual decorations such as small boxes wrapped in pretty paper as "presents."

Nature's own. Collect dry seedpods from your lawn, the park, or a fall garden. Save your nectarine, apricot, peach, and plum pits.

Decorating Techniques

Use these basic decorating techniques to create a variety of wreaths.

Flowery bowery. Use fresh flowers (watch them droop and dry and still be beautiful) or flowers dried properly with silica gel or very dry sand. Just layer the flowers (roses and zinnias work well) carefully in the gel or sand so they don't touch each other. Then, cover the container tightly. Check the flowers in a few days; then tie and glue them onto your wreath.

Recycled wreaths. Use various recyclable materials such as yarn, beads, and red netting "bows" from fruit and vegetable bags. Attach ribbons and pretty papers from old presents, or make "flowers" out of plastic pull strips and colored plastic lids.

CORN HUSK FOLKS

Figures made of corncobs and corn husks were the earliest dolls made in the Americas. Since corn was the main grain of North and South America, all parts of the plant were used — the grain for food, the stalks for animal feed, the cobs for pipes, and the husks for bedding, baskets, and these simple dolls.

Easy-to-Make Folks

WHAT YOU NEED

- Corn husks (from corn-on-the-cob or a craft store)
- Corn silk (the "hairs" just under the husk)
- Fine yarn or embroidery thread for hair *(optional)*
- Thin wire or string, cut to 3" (7.5 cm) lengths, about 10
- Thick wire cut to 5" (12.5 cm) lengths, 1 per doll
- Glue sticks

1 to 2 hours

④ Fold down the husks so the tied part is now the top of the head. Smooth out one of the husks to form a face. Tie the neck 1" (2.5 cm) from the top tie.

⑤ To make bendable arms, wrap two 5" to 7" (12 to 18 cm) husks around a 5" (12 cm) wire and tie at both ends with thin wire.

⑥ Lift up half the husks to the neck and put the arms in between the front and back husks. Tie the husks where you want the waist to be.

WHAT YOU DO

① If using dried husks, soak them in water until flexible for about 20 minutes. For fresh husks, let air-dry for a few hours before starting.

② Tie together 3 to 5 of the longest and widest husks at the bottom (the nonpointed, thick end) with thin wire or string.

③ Trim off extra-long husks so they are about 7" (18 cm) long.

Cut

7"

Tie

From the Cornfield to the Dollhouse

Corn dolls were first made by the Iroquois of what is now New York State. They usually used the cob for the body and made clothes of husks or leather.

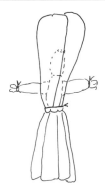

7 Make a skirt by placing several 8" to 10" (20 to 25 cm) husks in front of and behind the figure so they hide the head. Tie them at the waist.

8 Fold down the husk to form a skirt, or create pants by dividing the skirt into 2 legs, tying them at the ankles.

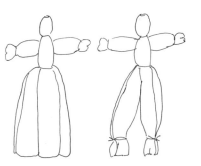

Hair for Husk Folks

- In step 2, put some corn silk in between the husks. Then, when you fold down the husks and tie at the neck, hair will come out the top of the head!

- If you unravel an old sweater or an old sock, you'll get some fun, curly yarn to use as hair.

9 Let dry in the sun, about 30 minutes, so the colors won't run when you draw the face.

10 Draw on the face with extra-fine-tip permanent markers. Glue on corn silk or use fine yarn or embroidery thread for hair.

WHAT YOU DO

1 Cut some husks into 1"-, $^1/_2$"-, and $^1/_4$-" (2.5 cm-, 1 cm-, and 5 mm-) wide strips.

2 Form a small ball of husk scraps for the head. Then, place the ball in the center of a 1"- (2.5 cm-) wide x 5"- (12.5 cm-) long strip that would make a smooth face.

3 Fold the strip over and tie it to form the neck.

Advanced Folks

4 To form the arms, insert a 5"- (12.5 cm-) thick flexible wire between the 2 strips under the head.

5 Starting at the "hand," wrap a 1"- (2.5 cm-) wide husk around one arm, across the chest, and down the other arm. Repeat with another husk strip if the wire is not completely covered. Tie at the wrists.

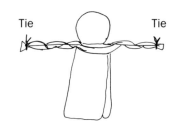

6 To make billowy arms, tie several $^1/_2$"- (1 cm-) wide husks around the wrist, away from the body. Fold them back, over the arm, and tie at the shoulder.

7 To make a bodice, start below the waist and bring two 1"- (2.5 cm-) wide strips across the chest, over the shoulder, and below the waist. Crisscross the 2 strips in front and back.

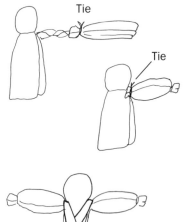

10 Let the figure dry in the sun, about 30 minutes, so the colors won't run when you draw the face.

11 Draw on the face with markers. Glue on corn silk or use fine yarn or embroidery thread for hair. Your beautiful doll will make a wonderful present or keepsake.

Scrappy Digs

Dress up Corn Husk Folks in "real" clothes. Cut calico, lace, ribbon, and other fabric scraps into pants, shirts, and skirts; then, tie or glue on the clothes.

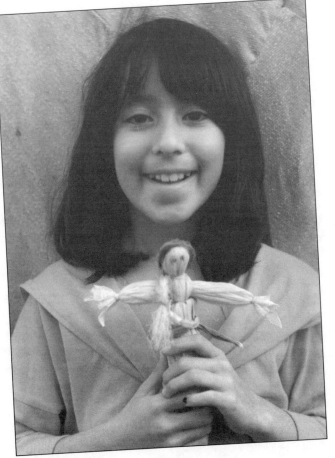

8 Make the skirt or pants (see Easy-to-Make Folks on pages 31–33).

9 Using a ¼"- (5 mm-) wide strip, cover the tie at the waist and make a bow in back.

APPLE TRICKS

Apples were brought to America from Europe, but they soon became a symbol of America. Apple trees did well in the severe New England climate and kept well over the winter, stored in barrels (which is where the saying "One rotten apple spoils the barrel" probably came from!). Ahead are some fun — and delicious — tricks, all with apples as the main attraction. Fake-out a friend with a Wormy Apple or sit your family down to a yummy Phony Apple Pie dessert — they'll actually thank you for it!

¹/₂ hour

Wormy Apple

This trick is great because of its nice surprise. It's also a great trick to play on your parents, your siblings, and your friends.

WHAT YOU NEED

- Apples
- Hot fudge sauce (or cocoa mix and a tiny amount of water)
- Potato peeler

1 Partially core the apple with a potato peeler, beginning at the flower (bottom) end. Scoop out the core about halfway up the apple. Save a piece of the skin and apple meat to replug the core hole.

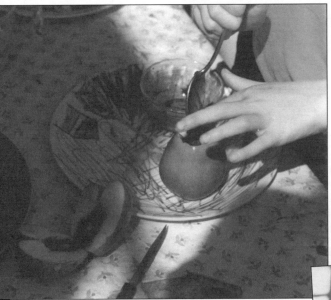

Flower end

2 Spoon hot fudge sauce or cocoa mix into the hole; then, plug the hole with the apple piece and skin.

3 Offer your "wormy" apple to an unsuspecting someone. When that person innocently bites the apple, he or she will be horrified by the decayed looking inside, but then pleasantly surprised by the delicious flavor. You might want to put a gummy worm in with the chocolate mush for a real surprise!

Old Tricksters

April Fools' Day is a favorite time to play tricks, but most people would like to play tricks more often. There's something peculiarly satisfying about tricks, and playing them on people is an age-old tradition. Many Native cultures have tricksters, like Coyote, who did things that were shocking and wicked. The Northwest Coast Natives have many stories about Raven, who is naughty, irresponsible, and tricky. So when you play tricks, you're continuing a long tradition!

1 1/2 hours

WHAT YOU NEED

- 2 piecrusts (available in grocery stores)
- 1 cup (250 ml) water
- 1 cup (250 ml) sugar
- Juice and grated rind of 1 lemon
- 25 Ritz® or similar crackers
- 1/2 t (2 ml) cinnamon
- Medium saucepan and mixing spoon

Phony Apple Pie

A bsolutely no apples are in this shockingly good pie. It looks like apple pie, but it tastes better!

WHAT YOU DO

❶ Mix the sugar and water in a saucepan; then have a grown-up help you bring the mixture to a boil. Stir to prevent burning.

❷ Add the lemon juice and rind. Let cool.

3 Break the crackers roughly into quarters and put them in the bottom of the piecrust.

4 Pour the water, sugar, and lemon mix over the crackers. Sprinkle on a little cinnamon.

5 Put on the top crust and press the edges with your fingers to seal.

6 Bake at 350°F (180°C) for 20 to 25 minutes. Serve the pie warm and watch people's expressions when you tell them there isn't a single apple in it!

Making Do

Tricking people with these "fake" pies is fun, but the idea for mock apple pies probably originated during hard times when people learned to make do with what they had. Sometimes crops would be poor because of drought or floods, and farming families invented ways to make meals out of only a few ingredients. To learn more about how people improvised meals during hard times, read the story *The Long Winter* by Laura Ingalls Wilder, in which Ma makes an "apple" pie out of a green pumpkin!

APPLE

*A*pple dolls are fun because you never know how the face you carve in your apple will look after it dries. And you won't need to worry about making the face perfect — the natural drying process does the work for you!

FACES

Making the Head

1 Begin by peeling an apple.

2 Cut a 1 $^1/_2$" (3.5 cm) length of cardboard tube. Use the peeler to partially core the apple, starting at the flower (bottom) end.

3 Insert the cardboard tube 1" (2.5 cm) into the hole where the core was.

WHAT YOU DO

WHAT YOU NEED

- 2 small or medium-size crispy apples (make 2 heads in case one becomes moldy)
- Round-headed pins or cloves for eyes
- Cardboard tube from a coat hanger
- Paring knife
- Potato peeler

4 Very carefully, carve a face. Almost any face will dry into a lovable shape. Repeat steps 1 through 4 for the second apple.

5 Place your carved apples on a rack or support them upright in jars so they'll dry evenly. Put them in a warm place to dry for 1 to 2 weeks. Or, if you have one, put them in a food dryer for 3 to 5 days.

6 Observe the amazing changes every day as your doll acquires its individual personality. Use your clean fingers to mold the face if you want to change it as it dries.

7 When the apple is dry, insert pins or cloves for eyes.

Native Dolls

Dolls with dried apple heads and corncob bodies were made by the Iroquois people of the northeastern United States. They fashioned their dolls from crab apples that were native in America.

Making the Body

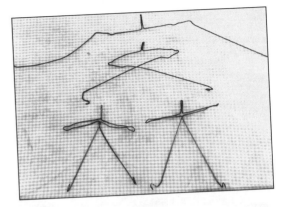

❶ Ask a grown-up to help you shape the body from coat hangers with the pliers. Straighten the neck 1" (2.5 cm) long, the legs 6" (15 cm) long, and bend the arms 3 1/2" (8.5 cm) long.

❷ Attach the head to the wire body by inserting the wire neck in the hollow tube in the head. You may have to trim the cardboard tube so the neck is a better length.

WHAT YOU NEED

- 1 coat hanger per figure
- Old sheet strips
- Cloth scraps from sewing projects or old clothes and socks
- Very small balloons (keep away from babies and toddlers, who may choke on them)
- Cotton batting or yarn for hair
- Pliers
- Needle and thread
- Glue stick or warm glue gun (with adult supervision)

❸ Wrap the wire frame with old sheets cut into 1"- (2.5 cm-) wide strips. Start at the foot and wind around and around, going up the leg, around the body, and down the arm. Repeat on the other side.

❹ Attach the hair by gluing on cotton batting or by using one of the 2 yarn hair methods (see Yarn Hair on page 44).

❺ Make clothes out of the cloth by gluing, sewing, or tying them on the figure. Bicycle inner tubes make interesting pants; old T-shirt cuffs, sweatshirts, and socks make great blouses and skirts. As always, use your imagination!

❻ Put very small balloons on the feet for shoes, boots, or socks.

Wrinkle in Time

How did someone first think to use apples for dolls' heads? In northern climates, where apples grow well, apples are kept for the winter in cellars. At first, the apples are crisp and smooth, but they gradually get softer and more wrinkled. Some people found ways to slow the process, but eventually, by the time spring came, all the apples would have begun to look like wizened, old people.

Yarn Hair

Method #1

1 Cut about 25 lengths of yarn 6" to 8" (15 to 20 cm) long.

2 Tie them together at the top, about 1" (2.5 cm) from the end.

3 Glue the hair to the top of the head so that the short ends form bangs. Braid the hair if you wish.

4 Make a hat or bandanna to cover the knot on top.

Method #2

1 Glue a long length of yarn, about 1 to 2 yards (1 to 2 m) on the head in a spiral so it covers the area where you want the hair and ends in the middle of the back of the head.

2 Make a bun with the excess yarn, or trim it off.

Kitchen Witches

In Scandinavia, kitchen witches are thought to bring you good luck in the kitchen. Without a kitchen witch, your bread and cake might not rise and your food will burn!

Make a broom out of a twig and dried grasses and attach your apple doll to it. Hang your witch in your kitchen for good luck, as is the custom in Europe.

KNOTS, WEAVES,

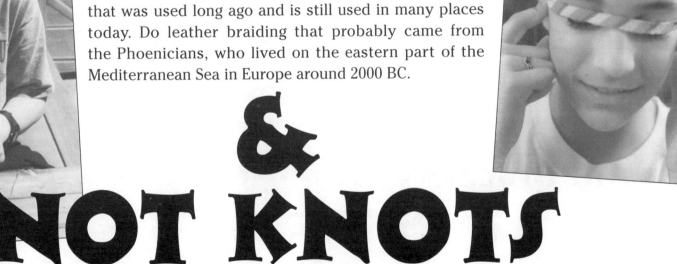

History is a long rope and you're the next knot in it! When you do these projects, you're using skills that have been handed down from generation to generation — for thousands of years! Make friendship bracelets like people do in Mexico, Guatemala, Japan, and all over the world. Create woven heart baskets — an old folk art of Scandinavia. Weave on a very simple, ancient loom that was used long ago and is still used in many places today. Do leather braiding that probably came from the Phoenicians, who lived on the eastern part of the Mediterranean Sea in Europe around 2000 BC.

& NOT KNOTS

ROUND

Why Doesn't My Goose

ROUND

F major
2-4 parts

1. Why does-n't my goose sing as well as thy goose.
Do Do Do Do So Mi Mi Mi Mi Mi Do

3. When I paid for my goose twice as much as thou?
So So So So So Do So Fa Mi Re Do

FRIENDSHIP BRACELET KNOTS

*I*n Japan, friendship bracelets are called wish bracelets, because you make a wish when you put the bracelet on. When the bracelet wears out and falls off, your wish comes true!

Level of challenge: 3

1 to 2 hours

6-Strand Bracelets

Note: You can use any colors you choose, but to learn the knots it will be easier if you use the colors I used for your first bracelets. It will make it easier to follow the directions.

WHAT YOU NEED

- Embroidery thread or acrylic yarn in many colors
- Scissors
- Pushpin, tape, or small safety pin

WHAT YOU DO

❶ Cut 6 strings of embroidery thread about 18" (50 cm) long or 4 times the length you want the bracelet to be.

❷ Decide on the order of colors for your bracelet. Knot the strings together at one end and attach with a pushpin to a table, or attach it to your shoelace with a safety pin.

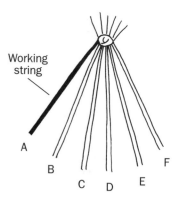

Working string

A
B
C   D   E
F

4 Repeat step 3 with the same working string (A) and the same underneath string (B). Always make 2 knots on each string. The knot will be the color of the working string because the underneath string is covered by the knot.

5 Repeat steps 3 and 4 with the same working string, but this time with the third string as the underneath string.

6 Continue across, using the same working string the whole time and knotting it twice over each color, until you have a diagonal stripe of the working string.

3 The string at the far left is always the working string, as shown. Take the working string (A) in one hand and hold the next string (B) firmly in the other. Make a knot shaped like a "4" by going across the red string and then back under it, and back across where you first crossed it. Pull the working string up to the top to make a tight knot.

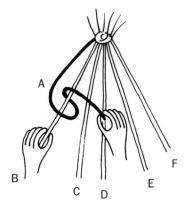

New working string

B C D E F A

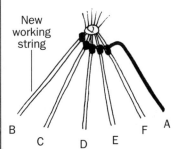

7 In the second row, the second string becomes the working string, because now it will be on the far left. For row 3, the third string will be the working string, and so on. Continue until you run out of string. Tie it on your own or a friend's wrist — don't forget to make a wish!

Bracelet-Making Tips

- Master the basic bracelet before trying variations such as "Vs," diamonds, and hearts (see the next page).
- Keep the threads from getting tangled at the bottom by stopping from time to time and sorting them out.
- The pattern will be uniform if you make each knot the same tightness.
- For an easy knotted bracelet, start with 3 strands.

Common Threads

Friendship bracelet knots, also called diagonal clove hitches, were used almost as long ago as rope for common tasks and probably also for decorative purposes. The knots we now use were probably from Guatemala, and brought to North America in the 1960s. Now kids the world over make them.

V-Design Bracelets

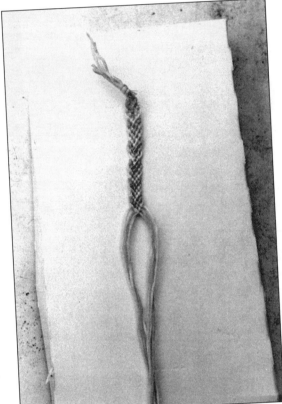

Begin these bracelets the same way you did the 6-strand bracelets, but use 2 strands each of only 3 colors. Use the colors as shown and you'll be able to follow these steps more easily.

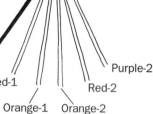

Purple-1   Purple-2
Red-1   Red-2
Orange-1   Orange-2

WHAT YOU DO

1 Knot purple-1 over red-1 twice; then, knot purple-1 over orange-1 twice, the same as in the basic process (see pages 46-47).

2 Knot purple-2 over red-2 twice with a backwards knot, the regular knot in reverse. Then, knot purple-2 over orange-2 with a backwards knot twice.

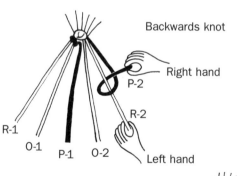

Backwards knot

Right hand
P-2
R-2
R-1
O-1   P-1   O-2   Left hand

3 Knot purple-2 over purple-1 with a regular knot twice. You have made your first V!

4 Repeat with red-1 and red-2. Repeat with orange-1 and orange-2. Continue until you run out of string.

R-1   R-2
O-1   O-2
P-1   P-2

Xs and Diamonds

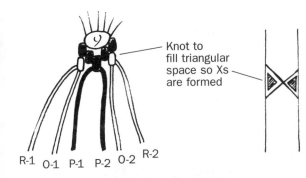

Knot to
fill triangular
space so Xs
are formed

R-1 O-1 P-1 P-2 O-2 R-2

WHAT YOU DO

1 Begin the same way as with the "Vs" (see page 48). Make one row of purple "Vs."

2 To fill in each triangle on the sides of the X, knot red-2 over orange-2 twice with a backwards knot; then, knot red-1 over orange-1 twice with a regular knot.

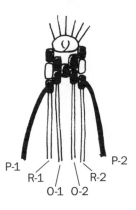

P-1   P-2
R-1 R-2
O-1 O-2

3 To make the bottom of the X, knot purple-2 over orange-2 twice with a regular knot. Then, knot purple-2 over red-2 twice with a regular knot. Knot purple-1 over orange-1 twice with a backwards knot. Then, knot purple-1 over red-1 twice with a backwards knot. You have made one X!

4 To make the center of the diamond, knot orange-1 over orange-2 twice with a regular knot. Knot orange-2 over red-2 twice with a regular knot. Knot orange-1 over red-1 twice with a backwards knot. Then, knot red-1 over red-2 twice with a regular knot.

5 Start at step 1 again. Make another "V" row and you now have one diamond. Keep going as long as you want!

P-1 O-1   O-2 P-2
R-1 R-2

Heart Bracelets
(12 strands)

If you're comfortable making the easier designs, you're ready to try this really nifty one. You don't have to use the suggested colors, but it will make it much easier to follow the steps if you make your first heart bracelet using 4 purple, 4 blue, and 4 green strands. You'll have to make several rows before you can see that the heart design is being created.

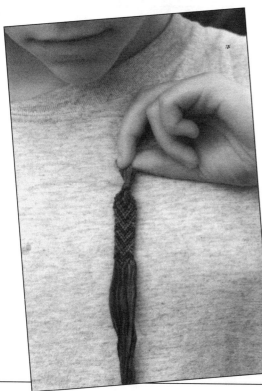

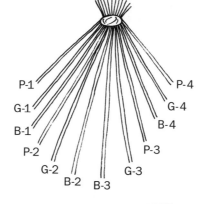

Purple-1
Green-1
Blue-1
Purple-2
Green-2
Blue-2
Blue-3
Green-3
Purple-3
Blue-4
Green-4
Purple-4

WHAT YOU DO

❶ **Right side triangle.** Knot blue-4 over green-4, with a regular knot twice. Then, knot blue-4 over purple-4, with a regular knot twice. Then, knot green-4 over purple-4, with a regular knot twice.

❷ **Left side triangle.** Knot blue-1 over green-1, with a backwards knot twice. Then, knot blue-1 over purple-1, with a backwards knot twice. Knot green-1 over purple-1, with a backwards knot twice.

❸ **Right top of heart.** Knot purple-3 over purple-4, with a regular knot twice. Then, knot purple-4 over green-4, with a regular knot twice. Knot purple-4 over blue-4, with a regular knot twice. Then, knot purple-3 over green-3, with a backwards knot twice. Knot purple-3 over blue-3, with a backwards knot twice.

❹ Left top of heart. Knot purple-1 over purple-2, with a regular knot twice. Then, knot purple-1 over green-1, with a backwards knot twice. Knot purple-1 over blue-1, with a backwards knot twice. Knot purple-2 over green-2, with a regular knot twice. Then, knot purple-2 over blue-2, with a regular knot twice. Knot purple-2 over purple-3, with a regular knot twice.

❺ 2 rows of Vs inside heart. Knot green-4 over green-3, then blue-3, then purple-3, each with a backwards knot twice. Then, knot green-1 over green-2, blue-2, purple-2, each with a regular knot twice. Then, knot green-1 over green-4, each with a regular knot twice. Repeat with blue-4 and blue-1 to make the second row.

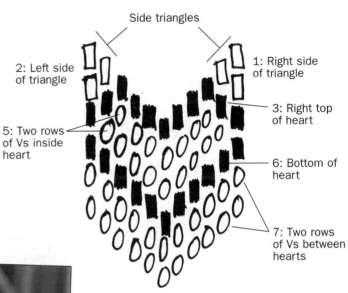

Side triangles

2: Left side of triangle

1: Right side of triangle

3: Right top of heart

5: Two rows of Vs inside heart

6: Bottom of heart

7: Two rows of Vs between hearts

❻ Bottom of heart. Knot purple-4 over green-3, blue-3, purple-3, green-4, blue-4, each with a backwards knot twice. Then, knot purple-1 over green-2, blue-2, purple-2, green-1, and blue-1; each with a regular knot twice. Then, knot purple-1 over purple-4, each with a regular knot twice.

❼ Make 2 rows of regular Vs before starting the next heart.

❽ Repeat from the beginning. Doesn't it look good?

KNOTS THAT ARE NOT

M*ake yourself a belt, a bracelet, or a choker using these surprising methods. You can braid leather without cutting through either end and you can make lacy yarn out of a single strand.*

WHAT YOU NEED

- 1"- (2.5 cm-) wide leather strip, about 1/3 longer than you want the final belt, neck-lace, or bracelet to be (if your wrist is 6" [15 cm] around, cut an 8" [20 cm] strip of leather; if your waist is 21" [52.5 cm], cut a 28" [70 cm] length strip of leather) (Ask leather shops, leather product manufactur-ers, and tanning companies for scraps.)
- Sharp scissors (for cutting thin leather)
- X-acto knife (for cutting thick leather, ask for grown-up help)
- Clothespin

Level of challenge: 2

⏳ 1/2 to 1 hour

Trick-Braided Leather

H*ere's an old cowboy technique that hasn't lost its magic!*

❶ Cut 2 long, evenly spaced slits in the leather strip, stopping about 1" (2.5 cm) from each end. Cut 2 notches near the top of the strip and an oval hole near the bottom so that later you can fasten the ends together.

❷ Start braiding from one end of the leather and braid it 6 times tightly (left to middle, right to middle, repeat 3 times). See Braiding Practice on page 54.

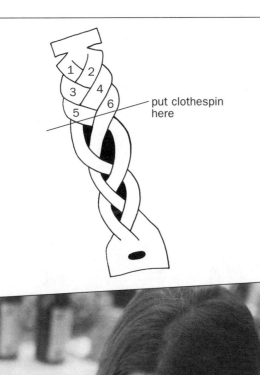

put clothespin here

Be a *Trenzador*

In North and South America, many intricate kinds of braids and knots were made by frontierspeople and cowboys for horse-riding equipment. You may not have a horse to make special stuff for, but you can still become a *trenzador* (that's Spanish for "braider"). The skill was brought from Spain in 1520 when Hernando Cortes came with horses and horse handlers to the Americas. Cortes was a famous Spanish conquistador, but did you know he was the first to introduce chocolate as a drink to Spain after learning of its tastiness from Montezuma, the Emperor of the Aztecs?

❸ Because the ends are not loose as in regular braiding, they can be difficult to untangle. To make untangling easier, put a clothespin firmly on the end of the braided part to make sure you don't accidentally undo the braids that you want. Then, feed the bottom end through the slits and untwist the leather until there are no more tangles.

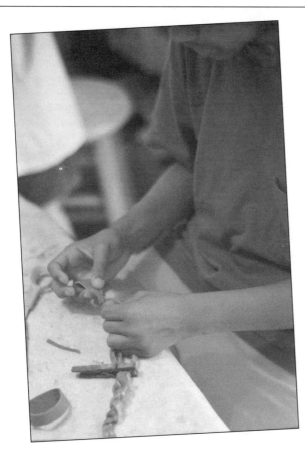

4 Braid 6 more times and untangle again. Make the braiding as tight as you can, because you always need space at the bottom to untangle after each braid.

5 When you run out of room, loosen the tight braiding so it fills the space evenly.

6 When you're finished, put the notched end into the oval end to fasten your belt, bracelet, or necklace.

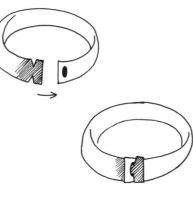

Braiding Practice

1 Tie 3 pieces of rope together at one end and place them on a table.

2 Take the far left piece and bring it to the middle. Then, take the far right piece and bring it to the middle.

3 Repeat left to middle, right to middle.

15 minutes

Cat's Tail Finger Knitting

*A*ll you need for this easy knitting project is yarn and your fingers. As you finger knit, you'll be using the same technique that the first knitters in ancient Egypt and Peru used!

WHAT YOU NEED

- One long piece of yarn (it can be connected to a whole ball of yarn if you don't want to worry about running out!)

WHAT YOU DO

❶ Let 6" (15 cm) of yarn dangle down the back of your hand between your thumb and index finger. Wind the yarn over the index finger, under the next, over the next, and under and around the pinky finger.

❷ Then, go under the second finger, and over the third, and under and around the index finger. Repeat once more.

❸ Pull the bottom loop on each finger over the top loop. You have knitted 1 row.

4 Repeat the winding of the yarn, over and under the fingers from index finger to pinky and back again, and pull each bottom loop over the new top loop again.

5 Continue finger knitting the yarn to form a long "snake" trailing down the back of your hand. Pull down on the yarn dangling off the back of your hand to see how your knitting looks.

Pull bottom
loops up and
over the top
loops

Top loops

Palm

Bottom
loops

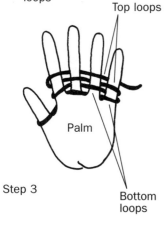

6 When you've finished, cut off the extra yarn and slip the end through all the loops, so it doesn't unravel. You can use the cat's tail for a belt, a choker, a bracelet, a ponytail holder, or a fancy tie for a present.

POPSICLE-STICK BELT LOOM

Looms are used around the world to make rugs, blankets, shawls, and wall decorations. Make your own small loom out of Popsicle sticks and then use it to create colorful belt or headband weavings.

WHAT YOU NEED

- Yarn (many colors) 15 to 60 yds (13.5 to 54 m)
- 8 to 15 Popsicle sticks, wooden coffee stirrers, or tongue depressors
- 4 wood pieces, about 8" x ¹/₄" (15 cm x 5 mm) for supports (or use tongue depressors or Popsicle sticks)
- White craft glue or warm glue gun
- Small cordless electric drill (use with grown-up help)
- Drill bits (about ¹/₈" [3 mm])
- C-clamp *(optional)*
- A strong belt or rope to go around your waist
- Yard- or meter stick

Drills Can Be Dangerous...

...so ask a grown-up to help you drill holes in the Popsicle sticks and always wear protective glasses when drilling. If you have a small cordless drill, have a grown-up teach you how to use it and how to set up a safe workplace.

Making the Loom

1 Mark the center of 8 to 15 Popsicle sticks (depending on how large you want your loom to be).

2 Ask a grown-up to help you drill a hole in the center of each stick, while holding it with a C-clamp or carefully with fingers. Use smaller drill bits for thinner sticks, and drill slowly and carefully to avoid cracking.

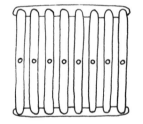

3 Place 2 of the support pieces on the table to form the top and bottom of the loom. Space the drilled sticks evenly along the supports. Be sure to leave spaces between each drilled stick; then glue on each stick.

4 Glue 2 more support sticks to the top and bottom support sticks. Let the glue harden completely (at least 1 hour if using white glue). Decorate your loom with colored pens or pencils.

Setting Up the Loom for Weaving

1 Cut the yarn in 1 to 2 yard (1 to 2 m) lengths. Use the yard- or meter stick to measure and cut yarn, cutting enough to have 1 piece for each slit and 1 for each hole.

2 Feed 1 strand of the same color yarn through each hole, using an opened paper clip to push the yarn through. When all the holes have a strand of yarn, tie the ends together loosely on each side of the loom.

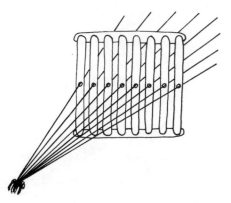

3 Now, feed 1 strand of the other color yarn through each slit.

4 Untangle all the ends and tie them all together tightly on each side of the loom.

Easy Weaves

To make the weaving easier, use one color of yarn for the slits and another color for the holes. Later, as you become more comfortable weaving, try working with more colors.

Warping Changes

When you put one color yarn through the holes and another color yarn through the slits, you get crosswise stripes. To get lengthwise stripes you need to put the same color yarn in the holes and slits that are next to each other. Can you figure out how to get a checkerboard pattern? See how many ways you can change the pattern by changing how you warp the loom.

Weaving

Right arm   Loom up

WHAT YOU DO

1 Attach 1 knotted end of the yarn to your belt. Tie the other yarn end to a doorknob, table leg, or a nail pounded in a handy place. If you want to be silly, tie the yarn to your toe!

2 Stand or sit back enough from the tied end to pull the yarn tight, so there's no slack.

3 Hold a small ball of yarn in one hand; then, pull the loom up with the other hand. The yarn in the slits will stay down while the yarn in the holes gets pulled up.

4 With one hand, help the yarn separate fully into alternating up and down threads, and then put the yarn ball through from left to right. Leave a few inches of the yarn end hanging out on the left side.

Fruit of the Loom

Guatemalan women use a similar-style loom to weave colorful strips of cloth. Their "back-strap" looms make strips about 6" (15 cm) wide. Sewn together they get wide cloth for clothing.

Colonial Americans used small portable looms almost like the one you're making. A boy could weave his own shoelaces and a girl might weave her own hair ribbons.

6 Pull the loom up again and use one hand to bring the previous row snugly up to the first row. Then, bring the ball of yarn through from left to right again. Continue alternating up and down and weaving back and forth with the ball of yarn.

7 When the woven part gets so long that you have to reach too far forward for comfort, roll the finished part up at your waist and move closer to the tied end.

8 When you've woven as far as you can, untie the knot from the far end and pull the loom off the yarn. Untie it from your belt and trim the ends. Be sure not to cut the ends too short, or the weaving might unravel.

9 Make small knots in the yarn ends. Save your loom to use again.

5 Push down the loom with one hand; then, use the other hand to separate the yarn fully and to push up the previous row snugly toward your waist. Bring the ball of yarn through from right to left until the yarn is even with the edge of the band on the right.

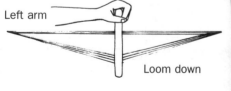

Left arm

Loom down

Weaving Changes

Can you figure out how to get only the warp (the lengthwise yarn) to show? Can you make both the warp and the weft (the widthwise yarn) show? It all depends on how tightly you pull the weft thread and how narrow you make the belt. Both ways make beautiful belts!

WOVEN PAPER HEART BASKET

T hese colorful baskets come from Denmark. The baskets are easy to make and can be filled with candy, dried flowers, or tiny toys and given as a present; or, leave them empty and hang as decorations.

WHAT YOU NEED

Any of the following:
- Good-quality paper: white and bright red
- Fronts of old, pretty greeting cards
- Other colors of paper or cloth

WHAT YOU DO

1 Cut 1 piece of each color paper to 3" x 10" (7.5 x 25 cm).

2 Fold the pieces in half widthwise and round out the ends farthest from the fold.

3 Starting at the folded end, draw 3 parallel lines about 3 1/2" (8.5 cm) deep.

Fold

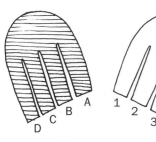
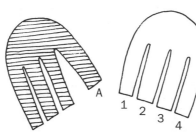

4 Cut on the lines to create 4 fingerlike sections. Do the same for the other paper.

5 Hold the pieces of paper as shown. For row 1, weave the top finger (A) on the left part into the 4 fingers on the right part. Go around #1, in the middle of #2, around #3, and in the middle of #4.

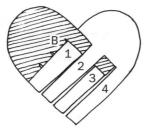

6 For row 2, weave the second finger (B) on the left into the 4 fingers on the right. Go in the middle of #1, around #2, in the middle of #3, and around #4. This is the opposite of how you wove row 1.

7 For rows 3 and 4, weave the same way as rows 1 and 2, using C and D to weave with.

8 Open your basket. If it doesn't open, you may have woven "in and out," instead of "in the middle and around." You can always carefully take it apart and weave it again.

9 Fill your basket, hang it on a tree, or give it as a present or a Valentine.

Valentine Mailbox

Make a big heart by using larger pieces of paper and making 9 parallel cuts on the fold. When the 10 fingers are woven together, you'll end up with 100 small squares!

MAKING YARN ROPE

For thousands of years people have used rope to catch things, hold things together, and build, carry, and lift things. You will probably come up with lots of uses for your rope just as your early ancestors did.

WHAT YOU NEED

- Yarn: a few yards (meters) of a few colors (odds and ends of yarn work well)
- A friend

WHAT YOU DO

1 Decide how long you want your rope to be; then, cut the yarn twice as long as that length. Cut at least 2 lengths of 2 or 3 colors of yarn. (Using different colors makes it easier to tell if you have twisted the yarn enough.)

2 Tie one end of the bundle of yarn to a post or doorknob. Hold the other end of the yarn bundle tightly and start twisting the yarn until the rope is very tight. Always twist in the same direction, and don't let go!

❸ Ask a friend to hold the twisted yarn firmly, halfway between you and the doorknob.

❹ Bring the end you've been twisting around to the tied end, keeping it straight and tight.

❺ Ask your helper to let go of the yarn and watch as it magically twists on itself. Help it to twist properly by pulling your hands down the length of the twist gently. Remove the yarn from the knob and tie knots at each end. You just discovered what makes rope so strong!

Fit to Be Tied

All the rope for the big sailing ships of the 1700s was made by hand in a method similar to this homemade yarn rope. First, a plant called hemp was spun in a clockwise direction into a kind of yarn; then, two yarn lengths were twisted together in a counter-clockwise direction into a strand. Three or more strands would then be twisted together clockwise to form rope. Rope is so strong because the twists in opposite directions catch onto each other and don't let go!

LEARNING

We're really fortunate to have the opportunity to learn things from many different cultures. People all over the world have the same needs, but each culture meets them in different ways — often with diverse and beautiful results. Because people move from one place to another and bring wonderful traditions and ideas with them, we're able to enjoy the variety of them, too. We can appreciate Jewish food by making delicious challah (see page 89), enjoy making and wearing Native American clothing like Tlingit moccasins (see page 82), celebrate Ukrainian and Mexican festivities by making Pysanky eggs (see page 94), piñatas (see page 70), and Mexican aluminum ornaments (see page 68). What a fabulous thing it is to enjoy our traditions and have the freedom to learn from and enjoy other people's traditions, too!

FROM OTHERS

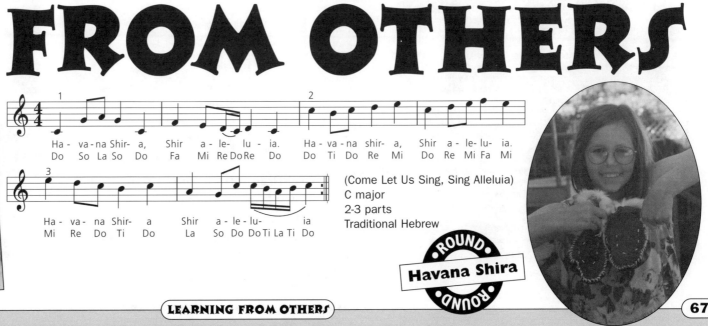

Ha- va- na Shir- a,   Shir a- le- lu- ia.
Do   So La So Do   Fa   Mi Re Do Re   Do

Ha- va- na shir- a,   Shir a- le- lu- ia.
Do   Ti Do Re Mi   Do   Re Mi Fa Mi

Ha- va- na Shir- a   Shir   a- le- lu- ia
Mi   Re Do Ti Do   La   So Do Do Ti La Ti Do

(Come Let Us Sing, Sing Alleluia)
C major
2-3 parts
Traditional Hebrew

ROUND · ROUND

Havana Shira

1 hour

MEXICAN ALUMINUM ORNAMENTS

These beautiful ornaments from Mexico are traditionally made from tin. Make yours out of heavy aluminum foil, which is easy to work with, and use them to decorate windows, the walls in a nursery, or the kitchen.

WHAT YOU NEED

- Aluminum foil roasting pans or pie pans
- Small piece of cardboard
- Wire or paper clips
- Scissors
- Nail
- Permanent pens: black and bright colors *(optional)*

WHAT YOU DO

❶ Draw a traditional shape or your own favorite shape of an animal or object on the aluminum. You might want to practice by drawing on paper first.

❷ Carefully cut out the design.

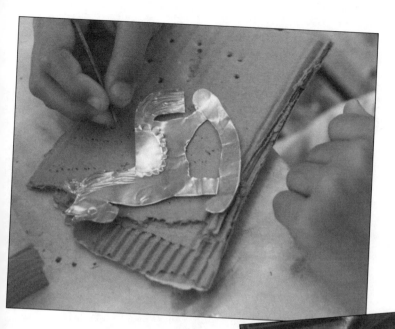

Learning to Improvise

In Mexico, many beautiful crafts are made from tin, in part because tin is inexpensive and easy to work with. Originally, the indigenous people (the Native Mexicans) used silver and gold to make their metal objects, but when the Spanish invaded Mexico in 1519 and took much of the valuable gold, the craftspeople and metalworkers

improvised by using tin. Since that time, Mexicans have continued using tin, making beautiful trays, pitchers, mirrors, and candelabras wonderfully decorated with birds, animals, flowers, and other shapes.

3 Place the cutout on a piece of cardboard for padding. Using a nail, make some impressions in the soft metal. Feathers and branches make nice designs.

4 Add color to the patterns with permanent pens if you wish.

5 With the nail, poke a small hole at the top of the ornament. Insert a wire hook for hanging.

Fun Frames

Make a few small ornaments (but without the holes for hanging) and glue them around the edge of a homemade cardboard picture frame. Glue a picture of you to the back of the frame so it shows through the front; then, give to someone you love.

PIÑATAS

*H*ave you ever taken a swing at a piñata?
When it breaks open — crack! — out comes
a surprise for all to share! You'll need to make
this in advance so it has time to dry properly, and
plan to work outdoors, as it can be a little messy.

1 week for entire process

Making the Piñata Form

WHAT YOU NEED

- Large balloons
- Newspapers
- 2 cups (500 ml) white flour
- 2 $^1/_2$ cups (625 ml) water
- Large plastic bag

WHAT YOU DO

1 Blow up a balloon and tie it.

2 Tear the newspaper (perpendicular to the writing) into long strips.

3 Put a big bowl inside a large plastic bag so that the outside and inside are lined with plastic. This will save a lot of time during clean-up. Mix the flour and water in the bowl with your hands. Squish out all the lumps until the mixture has the consistency of cake batter.

4 Wet the balloon with this gooey mixture and then spread newspaper strips on the balloon. Crisscross the strips for added strength. Add more of the mixture to the balloon as needed. Be sure to leave a 2"- (5 cm-) wide hole at the top for putting the filling in.

Note: Most people dip newspaper strips into the goo and then apply them to the balloon, which is actually a slower method. Try this new, faster way.

5 Continue until there are about 6 layers over every part of the balloon. Do the first double layer with regular newspaper, the next double layer with strips from the newspaper's pink section or the Sunday comics, and the last double layer with regular newspaper. The thicker you make the piñata, the more hits everyone will get when they are whacking it!

6 Let the piñata dry for about a week. After a couple of days, pop the balloon so the inside dries more quickly. If you really want to challenge your party guests, let it dry a week and then add 6 more layers.

7 When it's dry, fill the piñata (see Fabulous Fillings) and cover the hole with many layers of papier-mache. Let it dry for a few more days.

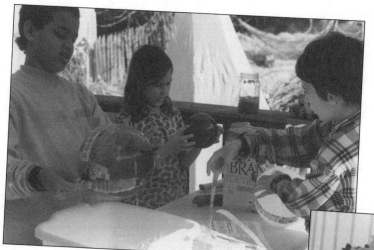

Fabulous Fillings

Besides candy, consider some of these fillings, or think up some of your own!

Traditional. Fill with peanuts (in shells), sugarcanes, apples, tangerines, and other fruits.

Party. Fill with unbreakable party favors such as kazoos, bouncy balls, Silly Putty®, paper horns, plastic teeth or lips.

April fools'. Fill the piñata with flour and act excited about the candy inside, while you give your victim lots of chances to hit the piñata.

Wet & wild surprise. In Spain, the piñata is sometimes made with a balloon filled with water—imagine the surprise to the guests when it breaks!

Treasure hunt. Fill with clues that lead your guests to a treasure such as the birthday cake or party favors.

Tips for Shaping the Piñata

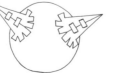

- Form your piñata using traditional shapes like stars, owls, parrots, and burros.

- To form legs, necks, or other straight, attached decorations, cut 1" (2.5 cm) slits around the bottom of a bath tissue or paper towel tube, bend the cardboard outward, and tape or glue to the piñata.

- **Starpoint cones.** Cut 2 quarter circles out of thin cardboard or thick paper. Masking tape the straight edges together to form a cone. Cut 1" (2.5 cm) slits in the bottom, bend outward, and tape or glue to the piñata.

- **Wings.** Use oblong pieces of thin cardboard.

Decorating the Piñata

Paint the piñata as creatively as you've shaped it. Acrylic and fabric paints work best, because they come in many shades and make beautiful and interesting combinations.

Traditional Fringe Design

WHAT YOU NEED

- Several colors of tissue paper
- Glue stick (not white craft glue which is too wet and makes the dye in the tissue paper run)

❶ Cut tissue paper in 3" x 30" (7.5 cm x 75 cm) pieces. (To make it easier, keep the paper folded as it comes in the package, and cut it every 3" [7.5 cm]. Then unfold it and keep each group of paper together for the next step.)

4 When you run out of gluey area, spread glue on the middle third of your piñata and continue the rows. Finish with the top third of your piñata.

5 Continue until you reach the top.

6 Glue fringe on legs, cones, and so on, starting at the bottom of the cone or leg.

2 Fold each group of 3" x 30" pieces lengthwise and make a 1" (2.5 cm) cut every $^{1}/_{2}$" (1 cm) along the strip.

3 Separate the fringe pieces from each other. Spread glue onto the lower third of your piñata and stick fringe pieces on one at a time, starting with the first piece at the bottom with the fringe down. Then, add another layer so the fringe overlaps enough to cover the fold of the layer before.

Breaking the Piñata Open

Attach a rope to the piñata so it can be lowered and raised as blindfolded guests attempt to break it with a large stick. Spin the blindfolded person around and around until he or she is disoriented; then, let him or her try to hit the piñata. Be sure to stand away from that person. Be sure everyone gets a turn!

Borrowed Traditions

Breaking piñatas is a Mexican tradition and a big part of the celebration of Christmas in Mexico. Piñatas were traditionally made with a clay pot covered with beautiful decorations. Before that, in Italy, *pignatta* (meaning "fragile pot") were pineapple-shaped pots filled with sweets that people broke at parties.

DREAM CATCHERS

D ream catchers are Native American good-luck charms traditionally made to protect children from bad dreams and to encourage good dreams. Bad dreams are big and prickly and will get caught in the hole, but good dreams will be able to slide right through!

Weaving the Web

❶ If the ring is unappealing, wind some yarn around it to cover it. Otherwise, tie one end of the yarn or string to the ring and wind it loosely back and forth across it 8 to 12 times until you're back to the beginning.

❷ When you get back to the first loop, put the yarn through that loop, but not around the outer ring. Continue around the circle, putting the yarn through each of the 8 to 12 loops in turn to make a web.

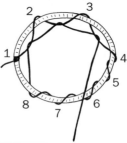

3 Continue around the ring again, going through the 8 to 12 new loops you created the last time around. Pull the yarn tight until there's only a small circular space left in the center. You may need to go around at least one more time if your ring is large.

4 Tie the end of the yarn securely, leaving a long end. You can attach beads or feathers or other interesting things to the yarn.

Wondrous Web Decorations

Here are a few ideas for making your dream catcher look special. Try them or think of your own wonderful decorating ideas!

• String small beads on the yarn as you form the web pattern.

• Tie yarn on the bottom of the ring and string beads on it, knotting the yarn at the bottom.

• Slide beads on feathers and glue the quills to the end of the yarn tied to the bottom of the ring.

Hoop and Pole

This Native American game is great fun to play, but takes good coordination to do well. The hoop was traditionally woven from a netting of rawhide, but you could use your sturdy dream catcher instead. To play, one person throws the hoop in the air or rolls it on the ground and the other tries to spear it while it's still moving, with a 12-yard (12 m) pole that tapers at one end (bamboo works well). The closer to the center it's speared, the higher the score (make up your own way of scoring).

Dream Catcher Earrings

After you make your dream catcher, try making tiny ones for earrings. You'll need a little plastic curtain ring or the cutoff circular end of a plastic bubble-blower wand, a blunt needle, and 18" (50 cm) of dental floss. If you use mint-flavored dental floss, you'll have good-smelling earrings! Loop around the outside 9 times and use the needle to help you feed the floss through the very tiny places. Decorate with tiny beads.

1 hour

IÑUPAQ YO-YO

M ake a toy that's similar to a useful tool. It's fun and furry and a challenge to play.

— 3 1/2" —

Basic shape

6 1/2"

Step 1

actual size

WHAT YOU NEED

- Two 3 1/2"x 6 1/2" (9 cm x 16 cm) pieces of fur (cut from worn-out sheepskin seat cover, fake fur, or strong cloth)
- Unpopped popcorn or other dry seeds
- An empty thread spool or 1" x 2" (2.5 cm x 5 cm) piece of wood with a hole
- Thread or dental floss
- 1 yd (1 m) rope or yarn (see Making Yarn Rope on page 65)
- Awl or hammer and nail (with grown-up help)
- Special leather-work needles or other strong needles for sewing leather
- Scissors

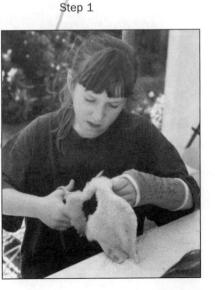

WHAT YOU DO

❶ For each yo-yo, trace the pattern 2 times on the back of the fur or fabric; then cut out.

❷ Working with one piece, fold the fur in half inside out and sew up one side.

❸ Securely sew one end of the rope to the top of the piece.

4 Turn the fur right-side out and stuff the inside with popcorn or small pebbles.

5 Sew the opening shut, knotting the thread securely.

6 Repeat steps 2 through 5 with the other piece and attach it to the other end of the rope.

7 Loop the yo-yo over your finger so that one of the weighted ends is about 3" (7.5 cm) lower than the other. Attach the handle to the rope by putting the loop at the top through the hole in the thread spool or piece of wood.

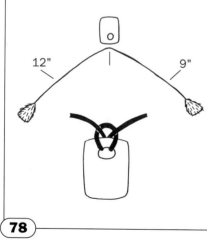

Playing with the Yo-Yo

*T*o *play with the yo-yo, try to get one weighted end to go whizzing around clockwise and the other to go counterclockwise vertically in front of you.*

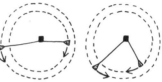

Method #1

1 Spread out the yo-yo on the ground or a bench.

2 Lift up the handle quickly and evenly as you stand up.

3 Move your hand up and down slightly to keep the yo-yo moving.

MAKING COOL CRAFTS & AWESOME ART

Method #2

1 Hold the handle in your right hand.

2 With your left hand, throw the long end up so it goes clockwise in front of you. Keep it going by moving your right hand up and down slightly.

3 Get the short end going by holding it in your left hand and throwing it down at the same speed that the long one is going, but in the opposite direction. The 2 ends will whiz past each other as you continue to move your right hand up and down.

4 Keep trying! It takes a while to get good at this, but it's lots of fun when you do.

Old Ways of Hunting

Your yo-yo is very similar to a bola, an ancient hunting tool used by the Inuit to catch birds. Historically, Inuit children learned at a young age to catch ptarmigan (a big, beautiful, slow-moving bird) with the bola. The bola used by the Inuit of Point Hope, Alaska, had 7 egg-shaped pieces of bone or ivory and a duck feather handle.

Yo-Yo Add-Ons

The traditional Inuit yo-yo is made of sealskin filled with moss and decorated with fringes of hide. You could sew some 1" to 2" (2.5 to 5 cm) fringes of leather or yarn on your yo-yo and watch them wiggle in the breeze as you twirl it.

Or, make the furry ends into creatures by gluing or sewing on features. Add moving doll's eyes that will "look around" as the yo-yo whizzes past you!

Ancient Toys

When you hear the word *yo-yo*, you probably think of the wheel of string you roll up and down from your finger. The word *yo-yo* was coined in 1920 in America, but the toy has been around for much longer. In fact, yo-yos were played with by kids in ancient Egypt 5,000 years ago! Since then, playing yo-yo has become popular all over the world.

NATIVE AMERICAN MOCCASINS

*M*ake yourself comfortable footwear that will fit you perfectly and allow you to walk silently.

Western Dakota Moccasins

*T*hese are easy one-piece moccasins, made in a way that may surprise you.

WHAT YOU NEED

- Leather (ask for scraps from a tannery, leather store, or craft store) or Naugahyde (vinyl)
- Paper grocery bag or large piece of paper folded in half
- Dental floss or yarn
- Scissors
- Pencil and ruler
- Awl or hammer and nail (with grown-up help)
- Special leather-work needles, or other strong sewing needles
- Clothespin

WHAT YOU DO

Making the Pattern and Cutting Out the Leather

1 Mark ¹/₂" (1 cm) in from the folded edge on the bag or paper.

2 Place your foot so the instep (inner side) is nearest the fold and no part of your foot is closer than ¹/₂" (1 cm) to any side. Trace around your foot by holding the pencil vertically, so you get the actual size of your foot.

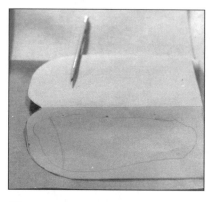

3 Label which foot it is; then, repeat for the other foot, using a second piece of paper, if necessary.

4 Because your foot is 3-dimensional, you need to make the pattern longer and wider than your footprint by drawing a line 1" (2.5 cm) above your toes, 1" (2.5 cm) below your heel, and 1" (2.5 cm) wider on the sides. Make the heel square, as shown.

5 Cut the paper pattern, being careful not to cut the fold; open the pattern. Place it on the leather or vinyl and trace it with a pencil or pen. Cut the leather or vinyl with scissors.

Sewing It All Up

For an easier way to sew through tough vinyl or thick leather, ask a grown-up to help you first make holes for the stitches with an awl or hammer and nail.

1 Fold the leather with the right side out and, using an overhand stitch, sew around the toe and down the side, but not across the bottom.

2 Cut a slit in the top side of the moccasin, parallel to the fold and the sewn seam. The slit will be the opening for your foot!

1

2

Step 4

Sew heel

1"

Cut a 1" slit 1" up from bottom

1"

Tlingit-Style Moccasins

*M*ake yourself a pair of moccasins just like *those worn by the Tlingits of Alaska.*

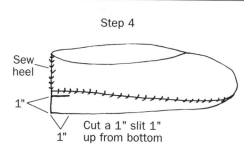

❸ Try on the shoe to measure where to sew the heel. Use a clothespin to hold the heel seam; then, take off the shoe and mark with pencil where the seam should be. Cut off excess leather and sew the heel seam from the top down to 1" (2.5 cm) from the bottom.

❹ Cut a 1" (2.5 cm) slit; then, fold down the heel and sew across the bottom. Cut fringe into the flap that hangs down. In traditional style, the fringe is supposed to erase your tracks as you walk!

❺ Try on your moccasins. If they're tight, cut the slit opening on top a little more. To decorate, see Adding Beads on page 84.

Step 4

WHAT YOU NEED

- This project uses the same materials and supplies as the Western Dakota Moccasins (see page 80)
- Tracing paper
- Safety pins *(optional)*
- Felt pieces

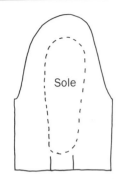

Making the Pattern and Cutting Out the Leather

1 Draw the moccasin bottom pattern shown here and see if it fits your foot. It needs to be about 1" (2.5 cm) longer than your foot and about 1" (2.5 cm) wider on each side. If your foot is larger or smaller, you need to make the pattern bigger or smaller, but keep the same general shape. Cut out your correct pattern on the paper bag.

2 Trace your personalized pattern onto the vinyl or leather and cut it out carefully.

3 Draw the vamp (moccasin top) pattern and make the vamp slightly larger or smaller if necessary. You can make the vamp out of leather or vinyl, but if you use felt, it is much easier to decorate it with tiny beads.

Note: If you are planning to decorate the vamp, do that before sewing the moccasin together!

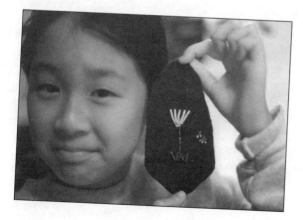

Sewing It All Together

An easier way to sew through tough vinyl or thick leather is to first make holes for the stitches with an awl or hammer and nail. Then it's easy to stitch the sides together.

1 Hold the vamp in place on the moccasin bottom by connecting the A, B, C, D, E on the vamp to the A, B, C, D, E on the moccasin bottom with knots or safety pins.

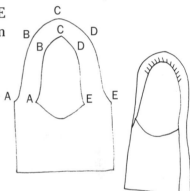

2 Using an overhand stitch, sew between A and B without gathering; then, sew between B and D, gathering the toe to fit. With each gathering stitch, make a small tuck in the sole piece. Then, sew between D and E without gathering and make a strong knot at the end.

3 Try on the shoe so you can measure where to sew the heel. Use a clothespin to hold the heel seam, take off the shoe and mark with pencil where the seam should be. Cut off excess leather and sew the heel seam from the top down to 1" (2.5 cm) from the bottom.

Ways of Life

The Tlingit people live in what is now Southeastern Alaska, and are known for their beautiful wood carvings (masks and totem poles), intricate baskets and clothing, and wonderful dances and songs. Alaska gets cold in the winter, but the Tlingit, who live along the water, on the many islands and inland passages, have enjoyed a plentiful and wonderful life through the years. The food from the sea is so bountiful that they have plenty of time for artistic expression.

4 Cut a 1" (2.5 cm) slit; then, fold the heel down and sew across the bottom. Cut the flap that hangs down into a fringe. The fringe is supposed to erase your tracks as you walk!

1" — Slit

1"

Step 3

Step 4

1"

—2"—

Adding Beads to Your Moccasins

To sew beads on the felt vamp (top) or on thin vinyl, use a beading needle, which is very thin and can pass through tiny beads. You'll need to be careful as you push the needle through the vinyl; you may find it easier to bead on a piece of felt that can be glued or sewn onto the vinyl.

WHAT YOU NEED

- Tiny beads
- Thread
- Pencil
- Beading needle (very long and thin)

You can put beads on your felt top (vamp) for the Tlingit moccasins, or on pieces of felt that you cut out and glue onto your Western Dakota moccasins.

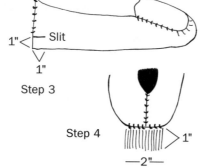

WHAT YOU DO

1 Plan out your design and draw it lightly on the felt in pencil (use white pencil for dark felt).

2 Knot the end of your double thread and sew through from the back, so the needle comes out where you want to start your design. Slip 3 to 5 beads on the needle and slide them down the thread to the felt. Place them along the design and see how far they go; then, put the needle through the felt exactly where they end. Bring the needle up through the felt before adding more beads.

Quills and Beads

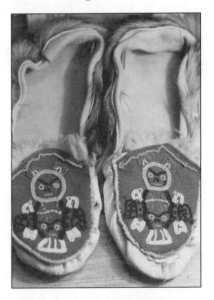

Native Americans have been respected for their beautiful beadwork. Originally they created beautiful designs on moccasins with porcupine quills. But when westerners gave them beads during times of trading, they rejoiced in the beads' bright colors, and made their traditional designs with the new material. Present-day Tlingit people make eagles, frogs, and other animal designs.

Adding Fur to Your Moccasins

WHAT YOU NEED

• Fake fur, $1/2$"- (1 cm-) wide strips

WHAT YOU DO

❶ Decide where you want to place the fur; then, measure how much you need. Cut out fur strips long enough to cover these areas.

❷ Sew on the strips with an overhand stitch.

❸ Put your moccasins on your feet and dance around.

Rainproof Moccasins

Some Native American footwear has thin strips of leather sewn in between the two layers of each seam to make them waterproof. As the stitches are pulled tight, the thin strip gets squished and it fills in all the spaces. This eliminates the little cracks where water might seep in. The traditional method requires sewing through 3 thicknesses, so you might want to keep it simple and just stay out of the rain!

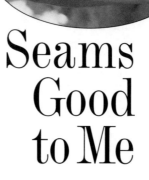

Seams Good to Me

You may notice that with both these styles of moccasin, the seam between the sole and the top of the shoe does not touch the ground when you walk. This is so the seam threads don't get worn out by rubbing on the ground. Can you think of any other advantages of this? Do you think it makes them more comfortable?

NATIVE AMERICAN DICE

This game comes from the Native California foothills group the Sierra Mewuk, who used black walnuts filled with charcoal-darkened pitch. Similar games were played all over America. The Iroquois people in what is now New York State played a similar game with plum stones that were painted dark on one side.

Making the Dice

WHAT YOU DO

WHAT YOU NEED

- 6 walnut shell halves (black walnuts are traditional)
- Nail
- Wax or clay (black wax from cheese wrapping is perfect)
- Small shell fragments, pebbles, or seed beads
- Sandpaper

❶ With a nail, pick out any walnut meat still in the shell.

❷ Sand the shells to smooth out any sharp parts.

❸ Fill the indentation with wax or clay, flattening the top.

❹ Decorate the filling with shell pieces, rocks, and seed beads.

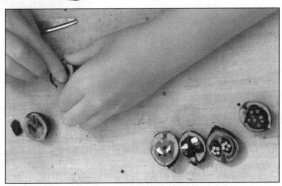

Making the Counters

Y*ou'll need 10 twigs or Popsicle sticks, about 10" (25 cm) long, per person.*

Carefully cut off sections of bark on the twigs with a penknife to form a design. Or, draw on peeled twigs or Popsicle sticks with permanent pens. Simple geometrical designs (dots and diagonal lines) were traditional, but you can use any design you like.

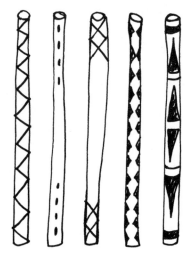

Playing

❶ Each person starts with 10 counting sticks each.

❷ The first player shakes and tosses the 6 dice. The scoring depends on how the dice land (see Keeping Score). The player collects the number of sticks indicated from the other player.

❸ The second player repeats the process.

❹ Continue until one player has all the sticks. It can take quite a while, as each person's fortune rises and falls unpredictably!

Keeping Score

In real gambling, each counting stick would represent something valuable, like one tanned skin. But it's also fun to play when nothing is at stake!

2 points (2 sticks) = All flat sides up or all flat sides down
1 point (1 stick) = Half up, half down
0 points = All other combinations

Many groups of Native Americans enjoy a guessing game in which two teams sit opposite each other, while one team hides a small object under a moccasin, or in one of the team member's hands. The other team tries to guess where the object is. The whole team gets involved by waving their hands back and forth with everyone passing the object — or pretending to — back and forth. The other team watches carefully for glimpses of the object. Then, when they decide to guess, they point at the

A Game of Guess

hand or moccasin where they believe the object is hidden, and the other team opens it. These games were sometimes used to tell if there would be a good crop, or used to resolve disagreements in a way that was enjoyable for the group.

CHALLAH BREAD

Staff of Life

Bread is the basic food in many cultures, yet many of us have never made it ourselves. Do you think bread has to be store-bought to taste good? When you discover how good homemade fresh bread is, you'll want to make it again and again. Some grown-ups are afraid to make bread, because they think it's too tricky. Making challah is a great way to show them how easy it is.

C *hallah is the special braided bread made for the Jewish Sabbath, which starts at sunset each Friday night. The Sabbath, traditionally a day of peace and rest for the Jewish people, is a ritual at least 3,500 years old. At the time of the Jewish New Year (in the fall), challah is sometimes shaped into a crown and dipped in honey with the hope for a sweet and happy new year.*

3 to 4 hours

WHAT YOU DO

1 In the large bowl, combine the salt, sugar, oil, and lukewarm water. Make sure the water isn't too hot, or it will kill the yeast.

2 Add the yeast, stir once, and watch it grow for about 5 minutes.

3 Crack the egg into the large bowl. Add the flour and stir the mixture.

4 Put flour on your hands and a board — a clean cutting board works well. Scrape all the dough on the board and form a big ball. Knead the dough for 5 minutes (see Kneading Bread).

WHAT YOU NEED

Makes 1 loaf:
- Pinch of salt
- 2 tablespoons (25 ml) oil
- 2 tablespoons (25 ml) sugar
- $5/8$ cup (150 ml) lukewarm water
- 1 tablespoon (15 ml) yeast
- 1 egg plus 1 egg yolk
- $2\ 1/2$ cups (625 ml) unbleached white flour
- Sesame seeds and/or poppy seeds
- Large bowl
- Stirring spoon
- Cookie sheet
- Cloth to cover rising loaf
- Pastry brush

Kneading Bread

Press down with your palms and fingers into the center of the ball, fold the dough in half, rotate $1/4$ turn, and repeat. If it's too sticky, add a little extra flour.

5 Lightly oil the bowl and place the dough in it. Cover with a damp cloth and put in a warm spot until it's doubled in size (1 to 1 1/2 hours). Warm places for rising can include an oven with a pilot, a sunny window, a car in the sun with windows closed, or a table or chair next to the heater.

6 Punch down the dough so the air escapes and it's almost the size it was before you let it rise; then, divide it into 4 pieces.

7 Roll each piece with your hands so you have 4 long, narrow pieces of the same length. Pinch the pieces together at the top.

8 Braid the right strip over one strip, under one strip, and over the final strip. Take the next right strip and braid over, under, and over. Continue until the loaf is completely braided. Pinch the ends together.

Making Bread Is a Science

W heat is especially good for making bread. That's because it has a protein called gluten that makes the dough elastic. If you've ever seen someone twirl pizza dough and end up with a large, thin circle, you know how stretchy wheat dough can get. Kneading is important because it causes two proteins in flour (gliadin and glutenin) to join together and form gluten. Gluten is useful in bread making because elastic dough will expand and not fall down when the yeast forms little bubbles of carbon dioxide gas. You'll end up with a light loaf of bread rather than a rock-hard lump!

9 Gently place the loaf on an oiled cookie sheet. Let the dough rise again in a warm spot for $^1/_2$ to 1 hour.

10 Paint the egg yolk on the bread with a pastry brush. Sprinkle the seeds over the loaf.

11 Ask a grown-up to help you bake at 350°F (180°C) for 15 to 20 minutes. The bread should be golden brown and will sound hollow when you tap it on the bottom (but use pot holders — it's hot!). Eat the bread immediately while it's nice and warm.

Rise & Shine

Yeast plays an important role in baking bread. It produces little bubbles of carbon dioxide gas that make the bread rise, until it's killed when the bread is baked. When you buy yeast, it's dry and dormant. It's pretty amazing how it becomes active when you add warm water and sugar!

Hungry Yeast

Today you can find dry yeast in a grocery store, but not too long ago, people had to keep their own yeast alive. They didn't know how to dry out their yeast without killing it, so they kept a moist "sourdough starter." If properly cared for, a sourdough starter lasts forever and can be passed from generation to generation. Each starter develops its own special sour flavor from the various kinds of healthy yeasts in it. To keep yeast healthy and alive, you have to use a sourdough starter every week, or at least feed it with a cup of flour and a cup of water so it won't starve!

PYSANKY

T hese eggs (pronounced *peh-SAN-keh*) were originally made in Ukraine, a country between Russia, Romania, and Poland. They were traditionally made at Easter, but you can make them anytime all year.

EGGS

WHAT YOU NEED

- Eggs (Do not boil the eggs. They're made for decoration, not for eating.)
- Egg cartons
- Short candle
- Powdered dyes: strong, bright dyes from art supply store or from Pysanky kits, or regular Easter egg dyes
- Cotton swabs
- Kistka tool for applying wax in a fine line (see Making a Kistka on page 96)

WHAT YOU DO

1 Prepare the powdered dyes by mixing them with water in glass jars. The dyes will last for many years if they're kept sealed and cool.

2 Light the candle (keep long sleeves and long hair away from flame) and warm the nail (or funnel end) of the kistka.

3 Dip the nail head into the melted wax (or scoop up melted wax from the candle into the funnel end of the kistka).

MAKING COOL CRAFTS & AWESOME ART

The traditional order for using dyes is yellow, orange, red, blue, and black. (Feel free to experiment, but keep in mind that you should start with the lightest color and end with the darkest.)

6 Using a spoon, carefully lower the fragile egg into yellow dye and let it soak for 5 minutes.

7 Remove the egg and let it dry about 5 minutes. Then, apply wax to all the areas you want to remain yellow.

4 Quickly draw on the egg with a thin line of wax.

5 Redip the nail head in the melted wax (or scoop more melted wax into the funnel end and warm the point of the kistka) and draw on the egg with more wax. Put wax on all the places you want to be white on the finished egg.

8 Dye the egg in orange, again leaving it in the dye for 5 minutes. After the egg dries, apply wax to all the areas you want to stay orange. Use the same method to dye the egg in red, blue, and black.

9 When the egg has dried after the last color dye, hold it for a couple of seconds in front of the candle flame until the wax on that one part is melted. Then rub off the melted wax quickly and gently with a rag or tissue.

10 Continue melting the wax on other parts of the egg until it's completely removed. You now have a beautiful egg to give as a gift or to use as a decoration!

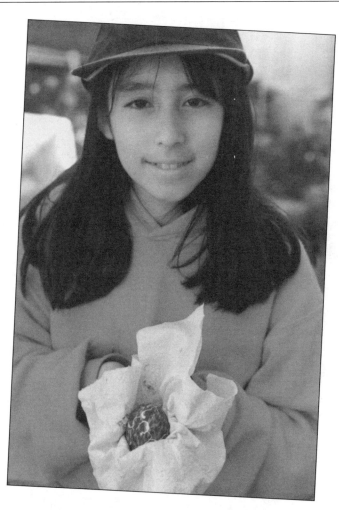

Making a Kistka

To make a kistka, you'll need a pencil with an eraser and a small nail. To use the kistka, push the nail into the eraser and dip the nail head in wax to draw on the egg.

Traditional Designs

Start with a basic design that divides the egg into evenly spaced sections. One tradition is to make endless lines of curlicues, waves, and zigzags that go around the egg and meet. Or, you might try using geometric designs like

triangles, which represent air, fire, and water; or sun, thunder, and bonfire to the Ukrainians! It's also traditional to make flowers, trees, wheat, vines, grapes, chickens, butterflies, spiders, horses, and deer. Those shapes symbolize good health, love, and wealth.

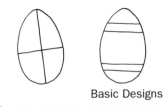

Basic Designs

MAKING COOL CRAFTS & AWESOME ART

Preserving the Egg

Traditional eggs still have the raw egg inside, but because the egg could go bad and cause an awful smell, it's a good idea to blow out the egg. You have to do this after all the dyeing is completed or else the empty egg will float in the dye or fill up with dye. You may want to practice on a couple of plain raw eggs first. Blow eggs outside over the soil or inside over a bowl or sink. Don't use the egg for food, because the dyes are poisonous and may have seeped inside.

WHAT YOU DO

1 Carefully prick a hole in each end of the egg with an opened paper clip, needle, or pin. Make one hole a little larger than the other.

2 Cut a drinking straw into 3 pieces and use one short straw piece to blow air into the smaller hole. You use the straw so your mouth doesn't touch the poisonous dye. Watch the gooey egg ooze out the larger hole!

3 Blow until the inside is empty. Let the egg dry inside and out.

Eggceptional Ideas

- Use large goose eggs instead of small chicken eggs. Ask for a supply at a nearby farm.
- Make a nest for your finished eggs out of cloth, feathers, foam, egg cartons, and small boxes.

Eggs of Glad Tidings

The tradition of decorating eggs extends back thousands of years in Ukraine, where decorated eggs were kept in the house to ensure a healthy family and to keep away evil spirits. Even now, each year at Easter, eggs are exchanged among friends and relatives. They are painstakingly decorated to express good wishes for the receiver. A young couple could be given eggs decorated with storks, chicks, hens, and roosters to help them start a new family, while a farmer would be given an egg with wheat shafts and farming tool shapes for good luck in the harvest.

NEW IDENTITIES

You probably love Halloween — not just for the candy, but also for the chance to wear costumes and try out new identities. Here are some fun things to create that'll make you look pretty different! Change your look with a new hat, a third leg, a misshapen head — even a "backwards" body! Another great way people the world over have changed their identities is by wearing masks. When you put on a mask, you may take on the characteristics of the mask and become wilder, more suave, sillier, ultraserious, smartalecky, thoughtful, scared, brave, babyish, or overly responsible. After all, it's all part of the fun of being someone new!

Let Simon's Beard Alone

ROUND

A minor
2-3 parts
Circa 1600s

Let Simon's beard a-lone a-lone, let Si-mon's beard a-lone. 'Tis
Mi Mi La Do Re Mi Fi So Fi Mi La La Do Re Mi La

no dis-grace to Si-mon's face for he had ne-ver one. Then
Do Do Mi Mi Fi So La Ti La So Do La La Si La La

mock not, nor scoff not, nor sneer not, not jeer not but rath-ther him be-moan. Let
So So La So So Re Mi Do Do Ti So Do La So Fa Mi Mi La Mi

FANTASTIC HATS

C reate and decorate hats that
amaze, astonish, astound, awe,
beautify, bedazzle, bewitch, bewil-
der, captivate, charm, confound,
delight, enchant, enthrall, fascinate,
flabbergast, intrigue, startle, stun,
surprise, and tickle your fancy!

Level of challenge: 1

1 hour

Foam Hats

I t's pretty silly to make a
hat out of foam rug padding,
but it works amazingly well,
because it naturally curves into
an attractive shape.

WHAT YOU NEED

- 9" x 12" (25 cm x 30 cm)
  flexible foam, ¹/₂" (1 cm) thick
- String
- Scissors
- Foam scraps (ask at a carpet
  shop for long strips of rug
  padding)

WHAT YOU DO

❶ Tie a string around the
crown of your head (the widest
part from front to back).

❷ Place the string in a circle
on the foam, at least 1" (2.5
cm) from the edge, and trace
around it.

❸ Cut a small hole in the circle's center and make about 12
cuts from the hole out to the
circle, evenly spaced around
the circle.

4 Trim the foam so it has a curved edge in the front and decorate the hat (see Decorating Hats on page 104), if you like.

5 Put on your hat, or trade hats with your friends and see how many ways you can wear each other's creations!

Not Your Usual Hat

If you made this hat out of buffalo hide, you would be making a sun visor like those made by the Native people on the American Plains.

Paper Plate Hats

This hat doesn't really shade you from the sun, but you can make a statement by wearing it!

WHAT YOU DO

1 Tie a string around the crown of your head (the widest part from front to back).

2 Place the string in a circle on the plate's center and trace around it. Fold the plate in half and cut along the line, leaving 1" (2.5 cm) uncut. The outer rim of the plate will be the hat brim, so don't cut through it (if you do, tape it back together).

3 Cut a silly shape on the center of the plate. When you put the hat on, this shape will stand up in front and look very silly! You could cut a heart, a star, or even a spiral snake.

4 Open the plate so the shape stands up; then, decorate it (see Decorating Hats on page 104).

5 Try on your hat!

1 hour

4 Remove the newspaper and trim the corners for a hat. You can make your hat any size at all.

Newspaper Hats

M*ake huge hats out of yesterday's newspapers. What a great way to recycle the funnies!*

WHAT YOU DO

1 Unfold the sheets of newspaper and stack them.

2 Place the sheets over your head, completely covering both front and back, and hold them in place around your neck (leave room to breathe!).

3 Have a friend wrap masking tape several times around your newspaper-covered head at the crown, just above your eyes.

WHAT YOU NEED

- 2 to 3 sheets of newspaper or newsprint
- Masking tape, at least 1" (2.5 cm) wide
- Stapler
- Scissors

5 Staple the newspaper edges together, or roll up the brim and staple it.

6 Decorate your hat however you like; then, try it on. Don't be surprised if people stop you on the street to get the news!

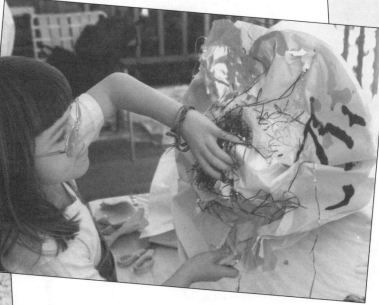

Wear It Well

Start a Hat Day tradition or host a hat contest. Give prizes for the biggest hat, the ugliest hat, the yummiest-looking edible hat, the best storytelling hat, or the hat that makes the funniest noise!

Decorating Hats

Decorate a hat you make yourself, an old hat from around your home (with permission, of course), or a big straw hat from a craft or discount store.

WHAT YOU NEED

- Acrylics or fabric paints
- Decorative items: yarn, buttons, felt pieces, lightweight items you've recycled
- White craft glue or cool-melt glue gun (see Glue Gun Safety on page 16)

WHAT YOU DO

Be as silly and inventive as you want. Paint your hat and glue anything or everything to it in any way you wish. Give your hat a theme by gluing on flowers or feathers, or decorate it for a special occasion like a birthday party or trip to the beach!

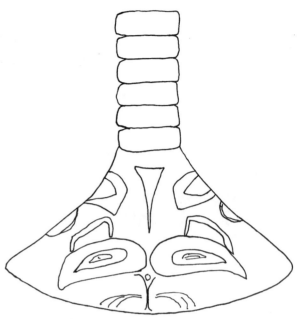

Share and Share Alike

Some northwestern Native Americans used hats as a way of showing status among them. Each time a chief gave a Potlatch (a huge festival at which gifts were given by the chief), he would add a new extension to his spruce root basket hat. These hats were elaborately woven out of thin roots of the spruce tree and decorated with wonderful art. At a Potlatch, the host would give away many presents and break his valued possessions to show off his wealth and to show how little he cared about those possessions, because he had so many more like them.

WHAT YOU NEED

- 15" x 17" (40 cm x 45 cm) foam rectangle, about 1/2" (1 cm) thick
- Acrylic paints (mix with water for easy painting on foam)
- White craft glue or cool-melt glue gun (see Glue Gun Safety on page 16)
- Stapler
- Rubber gloves
- Scissors

3-D MASKS

Masks are made all over the world and for many different purposes. In Africa, masks were made to express nature in all its wildness and exuberance. Many Native Americans made masks to represent animals and spirits, and sometimes used them to scare away bad spirits. In theater, masks transform the identities of people, sometimes from one gender to the other.

WHAT YOU DO

❶ Shape the edge of a large, flat foam rectangle by cutting away the corners.

❷ Make tucks around the edge by cutting 2"- (5 cm-) long slits around the edge of the foam where you want to make the chin, forehead, and cheeks.

❸ At each slit, overlap the foam about 1" (2.5 cm) and secure it with staples. Put a little glue over the staple ends to keep them from scratching you.

7 Cut other foam shapes for a nose, warts, a hat, horns, ears, or teeth, and glue them on.

8 Add color by painting your mask.

9 Because these masks aren't very comfortable to wear, glue a hanger on the back so you can hang it on a wall or door, or on a tree to scare away spirits.

4 Cut a mouth opening; then, make cuts above and below the mouth to bring out the nose and chin. Overlap the foam to form raised features and staple securely.

5 Cut eyeholes.

6 Glue on whiskers, eyebrows, and hair, if you like.

Hurt No Living Thing

Iroquois masks were carved directly on the tree, and were removed when partly completed. The Iroquois, of what is now New York State, were careful not to kill the tree and so used only one side of the tree. They carved scary, twisted, human-shaped masks to scare away the evil spirits they believed caused sickness.

1 hour

Jug Masks

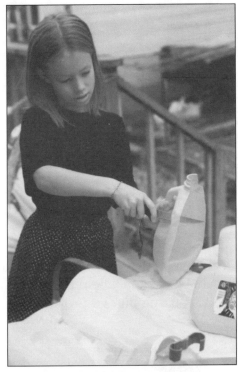

Alien

Carrot Top

Nosey One

WHAT YOU DO

❶ Cut the carton in half vertically with the handle in the center of one half. The half with the handle has a built-in nose for a mask, but the other half works well, too. You might also want to turn over the jug halves so the pouring spout is down, which makes a different shape of face.

Spacey

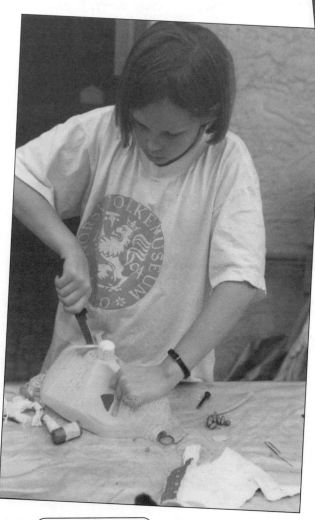

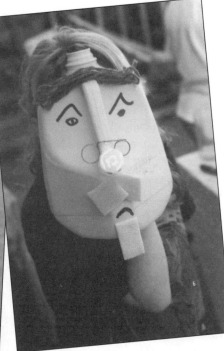

❷ To make facial features, glue on metal and plastic shapes you've collected from packaging and from reusable items (see Magnificent Mask Features on page 108).

❸ Use permanent pens to add details such as pupils and freckles, but be careful, because ink stains easily.

Magnificent Mask Features

Here are a few ideas to get you off and running, but ultimately the best mask features will come from your imagination!

More than two eyes. Cut eyeholes so you can wear the mask; then, add other eyes. For big eyes, use tin lids from juice cans; for huge eyes, use yogurt lids. Egg cartons make great bulgy eyes, and eyes on long stalks can be made by gluing plastic lids onto straws. Use feathers for eyebrows.

Nosing around. Use the top from a mustard squirt bottle or a zipper pull.

Big mouths. Use a broken zipper, a broken flashlight reflector, or parts of plastic packaging. Make a pipe out of a section of an old bicycle tube with the air valve attached.

Tangled hair. Use tangled yarn, wiggly wire, old pot scrubbers (cleaned thoroughly), or unwound, tangled cassette tape from old, unwanted tapes.

Beach Clean-Up Masks

Next time you go to the beach, make beach clean-up masks. Huge chunks of Styrofoam™, often found at the beach, make great giant heads. Decorate them with other found objects — and clean up the beach while you're at it! Remember, if you're always on the lookout for recyclable junk, you'll be ready to make spectacular unique art projects just about anywhere!

2 to 2 1/2 hours

LIFE MASKS OF PLASTER

Here's a mask you can make to fit your face exactly. In fact, no one else will be able to wear your mask. If you save it for a year, it won't even fit you anymore!

WHAT YOU NEED

- A partner
- Fast-setting plaster bandage material (from a medical supply store)
- Petroleum jelly
- Newspaper
- Old headbands or scarves, and bobby pins
- Hair dryer (needed in cool or damp weather only)

Feeling Comfortable

If you're a little nervous about putting something on your face that will turn rock hard, that's understandable! Maybe you have a friend who is more comfortable with the process who can go first. You help him or her with the mask and then decide if you feel comfortable having one made on your face. You can also make a partial

mask and cover only your chin, cheeks, and lips, or half of your face like the Phantom of the Opera!

WHAT YOU DO

1 Wrap a headband or scarf around your head so that all of your hair is away from your face. Use bobby pins to pull back every stray hair. Both you and your partner should wear smocks to protect your clothes.

2 Using a mirror, cover your face thoroughly with a thin layer of petroleum jelly. Be sure you include your eyebrows, up to the hairline on your forehead, under your chin, and on your eyelids, lips, and nostrils. Ask your partner to make sure you haven't missed a spot.

3 Meanwhile, your partner can cut the bandage material into 1/2" x 3" (1 cm x 7 cm) strips. Cut a big pile and keep them dry.

4 Ask your partner to moisten one strip at a time in lukewarm water, rubbing each a little to moisten the plaster; then, apply it to your face and smooth it gently with his or her fingers. Be sure your eyes, nose, and mouth are uncovered at the beginning so you're more comfortable.

5 Have your partner put strips on your nose and around your eyes. Decide if you want to close your eyes, mouth, and nose and have them covered. Cover under your chin toward the neck, but keep still and don't talk or the mask won't harden properly.

6 Have your partner crisscross the strips and apply several layers until it feels strong. Each strip should be smoothed into the mask thoroughly.

Feel the Heat

7 Let the mask harden on your face for about 5 to 8 minutes. It will warm up a little as it hardens.

8 Lean forward, holding the mask in your hands, and make lots of facial expressions (scrunch your face and wrinkle your forehead) to make the mask come off. If the weather is cool or damp, use a hair dryer to dry the mask while it's on your face and after removing it. Otherwise, it may not harden properly.

9 Place the mask carefully on a bed of wadded newspaper so it can finish hardening in the proper shape.

You may be asking yourself, "How does plaster harden and why does it heat up as it hardens?" It's all because of a chemical reaction. The chemicals in plaster stay separate until they are dissolved in water. But once dissolved, they react with each other and change chemically to a form that has less energy. The extra energy is released in the form of heat — which you feel as the mask hardens.

Decorating the Mask

WHAT YOU DO

❶ Add to the front of the mask (to make a bigger nose, add warts, and so on) with more strips of plaster bandage, but don't make any changes to the inside of the mask, or your face won't fit.

❷ Let the mask dry for at least 30 minutes.

❸ Paint the mask, if you wish.

❹ Glue on feathers, shells, sequins, glitter, rocks, seeds, eyes, ribbons, yarn, or whatever else inspires you. Remember, this mask can look as much or as little like your own face as you choose.

Plaster Masks for the Really Brave

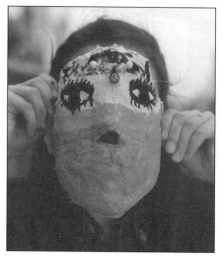

Some plaster masks are made by pouring liquid plaster directly on a person's face! The model lies down on his or her back, eyes closed, face well greased with petroleum jelly, and the face is prepared by putting straws up the nose and building "dams" around the hairline and under the chin. Then, plaster is ladled on thickly. When it's removed, this becomes the mold for the mask. Famous leaders or beautiful models might have their likeness saved this way and used for statues and mannequins. Some people even request a mask of plaster to be made right after they die!

1 hour

These elaborate feather masks are used for Mardi Gras in New Orleans. Mardi Gras is a wild celebration that's based on the ancient Roman festival Saturnalia. One good thing about those celebrations is that class ranks are often ignored and anyone can act like royalty. In Rome, it was a time when slaves and masters became equals. Even today, people enjoy dressing up as king and queen for a day!

WHAT YOU NEED

- Tracing paper
- Tagboard or a cereal box opened out
- Feathers (from outdoors, a craft store, or feather dusters)
- Sequins and glitter
- Ribbons, lace, or shoelaces, 1/2" (1 cm) wide
- Yarn or string
- Matte knife or small, pointed scissors (use with grown-up help)
- Craft glue or glue stick

MASQUERADE FEATHER-WORK MASKS

WHAT YOU DO

1 Make up a mask shape and draw it on cardboard. Cut out. If the cardboard is thin, glue 2 layers together.

Keep It Cheap

Buying a feather duster and taking it apart is a great, inexpensive way to get feathers for your mask. If you can't find one, you can buy the more expensive feathers that are sold separately at craft supply shops.

— 9" —

— 10"-12" —

Owl

Handheld party mask (glue tongue depressor to center of mask)

❷ Ask a grown-up to help you cut out eyeholes with the matte knife.

❸ Glue some feathers on the mask any way you wish. For a thickly covered mask, glue a first layer of feathers around the outside of the mask. Put the glue on the quill ends only, and let the feathery end extend beyond the cardboard. Then, glue the quill end of each successive layer of feathers so the feathery end covers the glued quills of the layer before. Use small feathers for the last layer, around the eyes.

Cassette Tape Masks

Make a fun handheld mask from the outside of a broken cassette tape! Paint and glue tiny things on one side; then, glue on a Popsicle stick to the back of one edge for a handle. Unwind the tape and use as hair.

4 Put extra glue around the eyeholes and sprinkle glitter or place sequins around the eye openings to cover up the last quills that were showing. You can also encircle the eyes with $1/2$"- (1 cm-) wide ribbons, lace, or pretty shoelaces.

5 Punch a hole in each side and knot a rubber band through each hole.

6 Use pieces of string or yarn tied to each rubber band to tie the mask around the back of your head. Or, glue a tongue depressor or Popsicle stick on the center of the mask as a handle. Now it's time to masquerade!

Mistaken Identity

You've probably read books or seen movies where the characters go to a masked ball to spy on or trick other characters in the story. Authors have thought of some wonderful plot twists involving mistaken identities. Watch a live production of William Shakespeare's *A Comedy of Errors*, or rent the movie *The Pink Panther*, to see how people use masks to disguise themselves. Can you trick anyone you know by wearing your mask or a costume (see pages 116-119)?

$^1/_2$ to 1 hour

SILLY COSTUMES

Anyone can buy a costume for Halloween or a costume party at the toy store. But here are ideas for some unique, homemade costumes you can guarantee no one else will be wearing!

WHAT YOU NEED

- Stick (to reach from elbow to ground) or an old metal curtain rod
- A sock that matches the socks you're wearing
- Wads of paper, rags, or pillow stuffing
- A pant leg that matches the pants you're wearing
- String, rubber bands, or tape
- 3 shoes that closely match
- Long coat (knee length or longer) with pockets, such as a bathrobe, lab coat, raincoat, choir robe, or old graduation gown

Three-Legged Character

Make a third leg and then walk, dance, and skip to confuse and amaze everyone. No matter what you do, it'll look funny, so have a blast!

WHAT YOU DO

1 Stuff the extra sock with paper, rags, or pillow stuffing and put one end of the stick or the curved end of the curtain rod into the heel of the sock. Pull the sock up and tape or tie it to the stick.

Character Costumes

Try these getups on for size!

The homemaker. Fluffy bathrobe, baggy pajamas, 3 pink, fluffy slippers, hair in curlers.

The mad scientist. White lab coat, pants that don't fit, nerdy shoes with broken and tied laces, uncombed hair, glasses taped at bridge of nose.

Cloak and dagger. Black overcoat, black pants, shiny black shoes, hat pulled down low, dark glasses.

❷ Tie or tape the pant leg to the stick. You can use a pant leg from a worn-out pair of pants that's cut off at the knee, or tie the extra leg of a pair of pants out of the way, around the top of the stick.

❸ Put 1 shoe on the fake leg and 2 on your feet. If your 3 shoes don't match exactly, use the non-matching shoe for one of your real feet, or use 3 different shoes so no one can tell which foot is phony.

❹ Put on the coat and slip the third leg under the coat. With your right or left hand in a pocket, hold the stick and make the leg move as naturally as possible. (Make the outside leg fake and the middle leg your real leg.) You will quickly get good at making your third leg look like it belongs there. Put both hands in your pockets to further confuse your audience.

Big Head

*Y*ou won't be able to stop laughing
at this cute, pudgy gnome!

WHAT YOU NEED

- Burlap bag or plain, old pillowcase
- Fabric paints
- Stick, about 4' to 5' (1 $\frac{1}{4}$ m to 1 $\frac{1}{2}$ m) long, or telescoping curtain rod
- Jacket
- Gloves
- Rubber bands

WHAT YOU DO

❶ Cut small holes in the top corners of the burlap bag or pillowcase for your fingers to stick out. (They'll become wiggly ears!)

❷ Paint a big face on the bag.

❸ Put the stick through the arms of the jacket.

Cut — Cut

4 Attach the gloves to both ends of the stick.

5 Work with a partner: One person puts on the jacket and fits the neck of the jacket around his or her waist. The other person zips or buttons the jacket.

6 The first person crosses his or her arms overhead and the partner slips the big head over the other's upper body, tucking it into the collar of the coat.

Watch Your Step

Have your partner lead you around, because you don't want to stumble or fall. You'll be able to see through the burlap, but if you fall, you won't be able to put your hands out to stop yourself.

Traditions Can Be Funny

The Native Plains Cheyenne had a tradition of the "contrary," where a religious clown sometimes did things backwards, including wearing clothes backwards and walking backwards. He fulfilled a serious religious position, but he also made a point of being as humorous as possible for the enjoyment of the group.

15 minutes

Turnabout is fair play with this very easy costume.

- Mask (see pages 105-112 or buy from a toy store)
- Dark glasses
- Tie or scarf
- Hat

About Face

WHAT YOU DO

1 Put your regular clothes on backwards.

2 Place the mask on the back of your head and cover your hairy "eyes" with dark glasses.

3 Put the tie or scarf on backwards so it goes down your back instead of your chest. You might want to tie it in front and then flip it around.

4 Now walk backwards.

5 To frighten trick-or-treaters or someone at the door, stand at the door backwards and then turn around to show your own "truly frightening" face!

2 hours on each of 2 days

ALTER-EGO SCARECROWS

Everywhere and in every time, people have had the same need to protect their crops from being eaten by birds at planting time and at harvesttime. Many cultures have made some sort of human figure to stand out in the field for them. Here are several versions guaranteed to keep the birds out of your garden!

Traditional Scarecrow

WHAT YOU DO

Making the Head

❶ Cut a circle in the sheet about 1 yard (1 m) in diameter, and fill the center with straw.

❷ Then, gather the edges and tie at the neck.

❸ Or, use an old, plain-colored pillowcase and take up the excess by taping or gluing a tuck in the back. (Pillowcases are too big and the head will look silly if you don't do this.) Stuff with straw.

WHAT YOU NEED

- Straw (wadded newspaper can be substituted for indoor scarecrow)
- Old clothes, hats, gloves, accessories (including glasses, costume jewelry, neckties, scarves, belts, shoes, brooms, tools)
- Yarn for hair (can use unraveled yarn from old, worn sweaters, see page 33)
- 2 straight sticks or bamboo, 6' to 7' (1 ³/₄ to 2 m) long and 2' to 3' (³/₄ to 1 m) long
- Twine or strong tape (*optional*)
- Rubber bands
- Safety pins or diaper pins
- Old sheet or pillowcase, off-white, tan, or light brown
- Fabric paint and/or fine-tip permanent marker pens, all colors
- Small paintbrushes
- Cool-melt glue gun (see Glue Gun Safety on page 16)
- Hammer (*optional*)

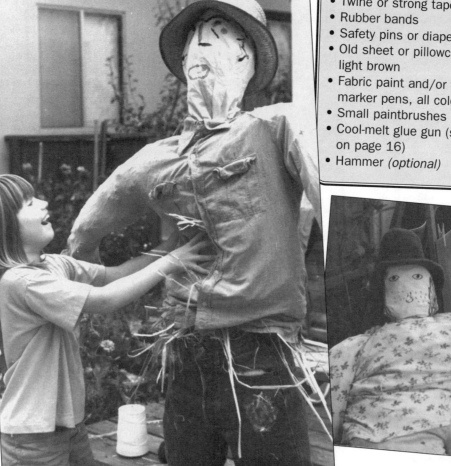

Painting

1 Paint a face on the front of the head, and let dry for 1 to 2 hours.

2 Paint colorful patches on old jeans and shirts if you like (with permission, of course), and let dry for 1 to 2 hours.

Assembling the Scarecrow

1 Put one pant leg on the long stick and stuff both legs with straw.

2 Hammer the stick with the pants into the ground securely, or place it flat on the ground.

3 Put the short stick through the sleeves of the shirt.

4 Put the shirt on the pole and tie the short stick firmly at right angles to the long stick using twine or strong tape. If you need to, ask a grown-up to help make this secure. Leave enough of the stick above the "shoulders" to attach the head and hat.

5 Stuff the shirt fully with straw; then, pin or glue the shirt to the pants in several places.

6 Add a belt made from a cloth strip, or use an old belt.

Scarecrows of the Past

*S*carecrows have been around a long time — as long ago as 2,500 years! Ancient Greeks carved scarecrows from wood and gave them ugly, twisted looking faces. Early Japanese scarecrows held a bow and arrow to make them look scary, and in Europe, early farmers made witchlike scarecrows.

7 Stuff the head with straw and put it in place. Tuck the neck into the shirt. Add yarn hair, a hat, and any other accessories you like.

8 Leave the straw as hands, or stuff some gloves and pin them to the shirt wrists. You can make hands or feet by drawing fingers or toes on stuffed white socks.

9 Let your scarecrow stand in your garden or on your lawn, porch, or front step.

Stuff It

- To make a scarecrow in a dress, stuff tights or pajama bottoms to form legs, use a long-sleeved T-shirt or pajama top to form arms, and then put the dress over them.

- To fill socks with straw, turn the socks inside out. With your hand inside the sock, tightly grab a handful of straw. With the other hand, peel the sock off your arm, over the handful of straw. Now the sock is right-side out and full of straw!

Scare Some Crows!

- Dress your scarecrow in big, billowy clothes and scarves so the wind makes them flap.

- Attach aluminum pie pans to the arms and legs so the wind makes your scarecrow clatter.

- Attach strings and netting from the scarecrow to the ground and trees so there's a bird-frightening tangle.

❶ Stuff the head and clothes with straw.

❷ Use safety pins to attach pants to shirts, head to shirt neck, pajama tops to pajama bottoms, and so on. Put dresses or skirts over the stuffed clothes, if you wish.

Soft-Sculpture Scarecrow

Y*ou don't need to use sticks to make your scarecrow stand up — you can make a big soft sculpture. It probably won't work in a cornfield like a traditional scarecrow, but if you have it sitting on your front porch — or lounging in a backyard tree — you'll certainly surprise the neighbors!*

Hold It Together

Use rubber bands to hold the wrists and ankles closed so the straw doesn't fall out while you're stuffing.

❸ Add hats, belts, neckties, gloves, jewelry, and glasses.

❹ Mold and shape your scarecrow's arms and legs to create the character and pose you want — sitting in a chair by the front door, lounging in the branches of a tree, or sitting like a hobo in the front yard!

Guardian of Fields

Scarecrows are found all over the world. That's because farmers from Asia to the Americas have had a common need to protect their crops. Their solutions for doing so, however, are very different. Early Egyptians, medieval Europeans, and Native Americans used real people to run and shout to scare away pesky birds. In Japan, some scarecrows were made of fish bones and rags set afire, and worked well because they were smelly. Nepalese farmers, on the other hand, wove dog shapes out of split bamboo, which guarded fields of corn growing at 10,000 feet (3,000 m) above sea level.

New Life for Leftovers

Here are a few ideas for using your remaining straw:

- Have straw fights.
- Build straw forts and burrow into straw piles.
- Read *On the Banks of Plum Creek* by Laura Ingalls Wilder, about sliding down straw stacks; then, jump into one yourself!
- When the straw starts to rot, use it as mulch for your garden or throw it on the compost pile!

CELEBRATE YOUR CREATIVITY!

You are unique and special, and your way of making things is different from anyone else's. These projects let you use your own special way of thinking and doing. There's no right answer or perfect example for you to follow — the more variety the better!

Every flip book (see page 126) you make will tell a different story, and the robot you'll create (see page 129) will have its own character. As you mold lumps of clay for claymation films (see page 132), you'll discover that each film production takes on a whole new life. Amazingly, just as every snowflake differs from the next, you'll see it's nearly impossible to duplicate the same design when making marbleized paper (see page 140) — but then, why would you want to?

Ahead you'll find some awesome, magical worlds to explore — from the inside of a Sugar Peek-In Egg (see page 135) to a cake with any scene your imagination could possibly dream up. All you need to do is gather some art supplies, put your creativity in high gear, and have fun!

Emily Fox
E minor
2-4 parts
Circa 1900s

ROUND ROUND

You Haven't Been Eating

You hav-en't been eat-ing   scall - oped po-ta - toes for three days,   like I have!
You hav-en't been eat-ing   cafe - teri - a lunch - es for six years,   like I have!
So Mi Fa So Fa Re   Mi Do Mi Re   Ti So La La   So La La

FLIP-BOOK ANIMATION

*C*reate your own fast-action story with paper, pencil, your thumb, and your imagination. Try sticking to simple drawings for each page at first; then, after you've drawn the main action on every page, you can go back and add more detail, background, and color.

WHAT YOU NEED

- 4" x 6" (10 cm x 15 cm) unlined notepads or 3" x 3" (7.5 cm x 7.5 cm) yellow Post-It™ notepads
- Pencils, pens, markers, crayons

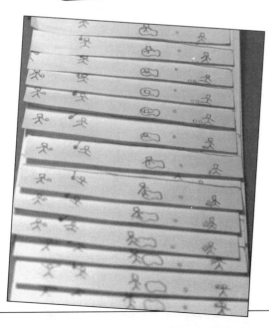

WHAT YOU DO

1 Think of a simple story that involves movement, but doesn't need words (see Ideas for Animation on page 127).

2 Draw a simple picture to start your story on the last page of the pad, near the bottom of the page. Draw the picture with dark lines so you can see it when you flip the page.

3 Flip to the next-to-last page and make a second drawing that continues the action of the first. Be sure the drawing isn't too different from the first, or the drawings will seem to skip around when you flip your book. This will be fairly easy, because you can see your previous drawing through the paper.

MAKING COOL CRAFTS & AWESOME ART

Ideas for Animation

1
2
3
4
5
6
7
8
9
10
11
12
13
14
15
16
17

- Balls bouncing and being thrown
- Drops of water falling and splashing
- People walking, dancing, or doing jumping jacks
- Plants growing, blooming, and dying

4 Flip forward from the back to the next page and make a third drawing, a little farther along in the action than the second drawing. Let the story unfold slowly. It will seem fast when the book is flipped.

5 Repeat at least 20 times, or until your story is done.

6 Flip through your book from back to front and watch your characters move!

Japanese *Anime* (AH-nee-meh)

In Japan, animation isn't just for kids' fairy tales; it's used for a wide variety of audiences. The stories vary in style and quality, but when they are good, they are very, very good. *My Neighbor Totoro* was dubbed and released in movie theaters in the United States recently. It's a wonderful movie, but it's even better to see the good *anime* in Japanese with subtitles. See if you can find it and these others at the local *anime* club or video store:

My Neighbor Totoro
Kiki's Delivery Service
Castle Cagliostro
Laputa: Castle in the Sky
Whisper of the Heart

Cartoon Creations

Originally animators had to redraw every scene when animating, just as you have done for your flip book. Today, it still takes many people to draw the movement of all the characters you would see in a Disney movie. Full-length Disney movies require as many as 65,000 pictures!

While animators still do much of their animation by hand, computers make the process much swifter. You may have noticed that animation quality really varies from movie to movie. It's not as interesting when the characters only change their mouth shape, but it is a lot easier to make.

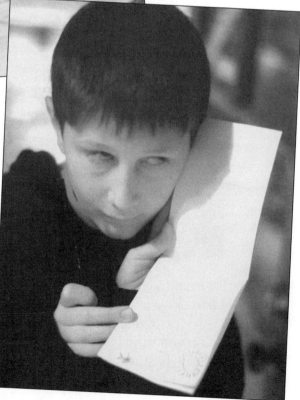

MAKING COOL CRAFTS & AWESOME ART

*T*hink of all the different robots you have seen in movies or on television. Some of them are funny, some are cute, some are helpful, and some are destructive. Robots are used in real life to do many tasks, from making cars in factories to helping doctors perform surgery! What kind of robot will you make?

ROBOTOLOGY

WHAT YOU NEED

- Recycled items for robot parts (see Robot Recyclables on page 131)
- Masking tape or wide silver tape
- Warm glue gun (see Glue Gun Safety on page 16)
- Scissors

WHAT YOU DO

1 Gather lots of material and find a large space to create your robot.

2 Rummage through your collected material for something to use for the robot's body. A medium-size box covered with aluminum foil works well.

3 Now, search for a head. Look at your pieces of packaging to see if they seem to have eyes, a nose, or a mouth. It's a lot like looking at clouds and seeing animals. You can accentuate the features with found materials, and add antennae, hair, and funny knobs.

4 Look again through your pile of materials for likely arms and legs. Yogurt containers make sturdy legs and worn-out car windshield wipers make excellent arms!

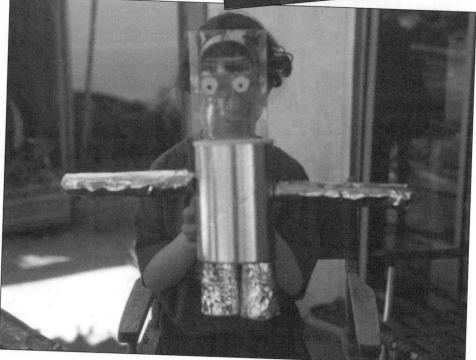

5 Glue and tape everything together so your robot will stand up.

6 It's fun to give your robot an electronic control panel in the front, with glued-on buttons and knobs. Use old parts from broken machines, corks, and bottle caps. You may want to make a remote control for your robot with buttons that tell what it would do.

Art in a Box

Starting an art box is a great idea. Find a big box and label it ROBOT. Then, keep your eye out for face-shaped and robot-shaped packaging and broken electronic things to put away in the box. Let the ROBOT box sit enticingly on a shelf until it's bulging with goodies; then, invite some friends over and let the excitement begin!

Robot Recyclables

Look around your home, school, and outdoors for recyclable items you can use for your robot and other craft projects. Here are some ideas:

Styrofoam™ packaging pieces

Plastic packaging in interesting shapes

Aluminum foil wrapping from cream cheese, candy bars, box tops (washed thoroughly)

Cardboard boxes of all sizes from food and drugstore purchases

Broken and unfixable household machine parts: telephones, tape recorders, remote control cars, old computers, floppy disks, watches, calculators, radios (ask for grown-up permission first)

Spiral binder edges (when paper is all used up)

Berry baskets

Corks, bottle caps, metal and plastic lids

Toilet paper and paper towel tubes, round oatmeal boxes

Wheels from broken toys or roller skates

Empty thread spools, tape spools

Robot Add-Ons

- Use foil to cover plastic and cardboard pieces to make them look like metal.
- Add wheels so your robot can move.
- After checking with a grown-up, take apart broken machines to get the "ingredients" for your robot. Never open any machine or appliance without first unplugging it. Consider a radio, old computer parts, a broken watch, or a remote control car that doesn't work. Don't just look at the outside, see what's happening inside! You may need a tiny screwdriver to reach into narrow spots where tiny screws hide.

CLAYMATION FILM

M ake your own claymation movie by creating a scene with toys, homemade playdough (see page 134), and your imagination. Make it move and tell a story, such as the "Monster Who Ate the Seafood Restaurant," the "Dinosaur Who Visited Our Classroom," or "Strange Things from the Sky"! Or, just see what develops. Your story may begin to unfold as you make the movie.

Level of challenge: 2

2 hours

WHAT YOU NEED

- Super-8 movie camera, film, and projector (ask friends, relatives, or neighbors, or check your local and state libraries' audiovisual loan department), or a video camera with animation capabilities
- Modeling clay or playdough (see page 134)
- Tripod stand for the camera
- White cloth or paper to cover the table
- Colored paper
- Cardboard boxes for backdrop (optional)
- Cotton balls for clouds (optional)
- Props for your animation: small stuffed animals, blocks, boats, cars, dinosaurs, Legos®, people, trains, town pieces, alphabet letters, clothespins, pinecones, rocks

WHAT YOU DO

❶ Begin by setting up your scene on a table. Use lamps to light the scene (don't rely on sunlight, because it will move while you are filming). Brighten your scene by covering the table with white cloth or paper to reflect light.

❷ Mount the camera securely on the tripod and set it on the single-frame setting. If your camera has an external push-button switch on a cable to advance each frame, use it. This prevents jerking of the camera, so you can animate the scene and click the frame advance without moving.

3 Center the camera on the table and focus on the area where your scene will be. Tape the edges of the area that the camera captures so you can keep the action in the camera's view.

4 If you want, make a backdrop for your scene using a rectangular cardboard box with one long side cut out so the camera can see into it. Decorate the sides with a scene.

5 Now, plan your story and choose your props.

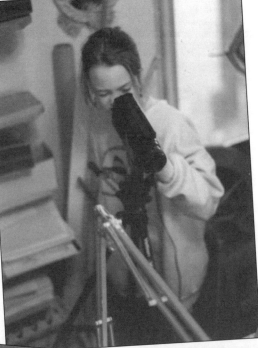

Using a Camcorder

It's possible to make an animation movie with a camcorder, even if it isn't an expensive one designed for animation. Try your camera out to make sure that you can take a really short shot and not get any "white snow" between each shot. With the camcorder you will be able to make your movie as long as you want, although the action will be more jerky. To film your scenes with the camcorder, you will press the ON button on and off as quickly as possible, once for each position of your objects. One nice thing about using the camcorder is that you can replay your film right away — there's no waiting involved!

Staying Focused

Keep your camera and your scene absolutely still; move only the action figures. Otherwise, you'll end up with a very jerky movie. Use clay or playdough to hold things in place, such as a car in a dinosaur's mouth or a tree on the side of a hill. Tie clear thread, fishing line, or even dental floss to objects so they look like they're flying, floating, or tilting. You or a friend can click the camera while the other holds things up with the thread.

6 Set the first scene; then, refocus the camera. Click about 10 single frames of the scene.

7 Begin changing the shape of the playdough slowly, moving objects about $1/2$" (5 mm) per move. Shoot 2 frames for each new position. More than one object can be moved each time, but try to keep the movement fairly simple.

8 To make a movie lasting 8 seconds, you'll need to make 67 different moves.

9 When you have finished your movie, have it processed at a photo shop. Then, in a week or two, you can watch your own movie. With a movie projector you can play your movie at different speeds, forward and backwards!

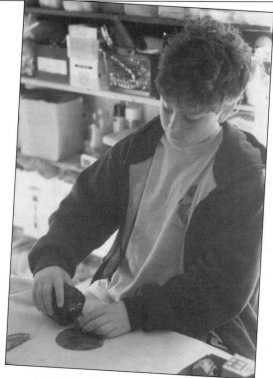

Super-Duper Scenes

- Make playdough go from being one kind of creature to another.
- Combine playdough and objects: Lumpy monsters swallow cars and buildings and then spit them out.
- Put moving eyes (from a fabric store) on playdough creatures.
- Objects appear or disappear "magically" when you put them in or take them out of a scene.
- Puzzles can seem to put themselves together.
- Cities made of blocks can build themselves, fall, and rebuild.

Playdough Recipe

WHAT YOU NEED

- 1 cup (250 ml) flour
- $1/2$ cup (125 ml) salt
- $1/2$ teaspoon (2 ml) cream of tartar
- 1 tablespoon (15 ml) cooking oil
- 1 cup (250 ml) water

WHAT YOU DO

1 Mix the flour, salt, and cream of tartar in a bowl.

2 Add the oil and water to the mixture.

3 Ask a grown-up to cook the mixture over low heat, stirring continuously until it is thick. Remove from heat.

4 Let the dough cool completely; then, knead it.

5 Divide the dough into sections and add a couple of drops of different food colors to each section.

MAGICAL SUGAR PEEK-IN EGGS

S ugar eggs are a traditional craft that originated in northern Europe. These magical eggs are fun to make year-round, not just in spring or at Easter. There's magic in creating a hard little egg out of crumbly sugar, and there's more magic when the scene is finished and you can peek into the miniature world you've created. Does yours look like a place you'd want to explore?

Level of challenge: ③

3 to 4 hours

Making and Shaping the Sugar Mix

T his recipe makes 5 big eggs or 15 small eggs. The shells are very delicate, so take your time and handle them gently.

WHAT YOU NEED

- 3" to 7" (7.5 cm to 17.5 cm) plastic egg-shaped mold (available in craft shops)
- 5" x 10" (12.5 cm x 25 cm) cardboard pieces
- Cookie sheet
- 5 lbs (2.2 kg) granulated sugar (for coarse sugar, whirl in a food processor or blender until finely ground)
- 2 egg whites (use powdered egg white mixed with water if you plan to eat your egg)
- Large mixing bowl and spoon

WHAT YOU DO

❶ Separate the egg whites from the yolks, and mix with the sugar in a large bowl by hand until the mix feels like wet sand. Use immediately, before it dries and hardens. Cover the remaining mix with a wet cloth to keep it damp.

❷ Clean and dry both sections of the mold.

③ Pack the molds very tightly with sugar; then, scrape off any excess sugar using the straight edge of a butter knife.

④ Place a piece of cardboard on the flat side of the sugar-filled mold. Turn the egg over quickly and place it on the cookie sheet.

⑤ Remove the plastic mold very carefully and inspect the egg to make sure it's smooth and uncracked. If it's imperfect, return the sugar to the bowl and try again.

Cutting the Peephole

WHAT YOU DO

① Ask a grown-up to cut off the last inch of the more pointed ends of each egg half with a knife. This will be the peephole you'll look into when the egg is done. Leave the cutoff end in place for now.

② Make as many top and bottom sets as you like, until the sugar is too dry to stay in the mold. (Save leftover sugar for baking.)

③ Let the sugar harden for 1 ½ hours, or ask a grown-up to bake it in an oven at 200°F (100°C) for 6 to 12 minutes. Check the hardness after 6 minutes of baking or 1 hour of setting. The outside should be crusty, and the inside soft enough to be scooped out.

④ Hold the hardened egg in one hand and use a spoon to scoop out the center, leaving about a ½" (1 cm) shell. Don't make the shell too thin or it may crack easily.

⑤ Leave the hollow egg halves to fully harden overnight.

❶ Fill each pastry bag or sandwich bag with a different color of icing. Secure the ends with rubber bands.

❷ Squeeze a little icing inside the bottom half of the egg. It will work as "glue" to anchor the candies where you want them. If you're using a sandwich bag, you can shape the icing with a fork or knife.

❸ Create a scene with the candies and icing. Remember to face things toward the peephole.

Decorating and Creating the Inside Scene

WHAT YOU NEED

- Small candies shaped like birds, bunnies, eggs, flowers, or trees
- Chocolate chips, jelly beans, jelly fruits, Red Hots®, sprinkles, or other small, colorful candies
- Granulated sugar, dyed with food coloring
- Pastry bags and decorating tips, one for each color (ask a grown-up to help you put the tips on), or sandwich bags with a small hole cut in one corner
- Icing, several light colors (see Colorful Icing on page 138)
- Red ribbons

Colorful Icing

Prepare this icing in advance and store tightly covered in the refrigerator. This recipe makes enough icing for 2 sugar eggs and fills 1 pastry bag. Be imaginative with your colors!

WHAT YOU NEED

- Food coloring, different colors
- 1 egg white (use powdered egg white mixed with water if you plan to eat your egg)
- 1 ⅓ cup (325 ml) confectioners' sugar
- Cream of tartar

WHAT YOU DO

❶ Combine the egg white, confectioners' sugar, and a pinch of cream of tartar in a mixing bowl.

❷ Ask a grown-up to help you beat it with an electric mixer until the icing is fluffy and smooth, about 7 to 10 minutes.

❸ Mix a few drops of 1 food color into each batch of icing.

❹ Make 1 batch each of light blue, pink, yellow, or other light colors.

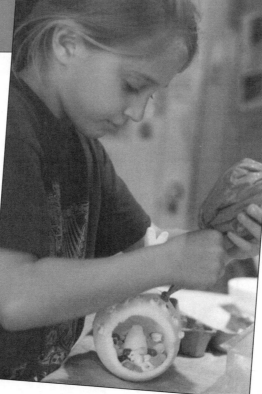

❹ Decorate the inside top of the egg as a ceiling or sky, but be sure not to overdecorate, as candies may fall off when the egg half is turned upside-down. Let the frosting harden completely before turning the egg over.

❺ Squeeze icing around the rim of the shell's bottom half and place the top half on it gently.

❻ Cover the outside seam with a pretty pattern of icing and candies; then, decorate the outside of the egg.

❼ Peek in! The little world you created will seem magically larger. The eggs will last for years if stored in a cool, dry place.

Little Worlds

Here are a few ideas for egg scenes to inspire you:

- A garden with bunnies gathered around a nest of eggs.
- A bunny at the beach with a blue-green icing ocean and brown sugar sand scattered with candy seashells. You can make a big sun on the egg's roof.
- A duck in a pond surrounded by candy flowers and trees. Make a candy path through the woods.
- An egg scene of Antarctica! Use blue sugar on the roof to make a glacier cave or underwater scene, and white frosting for snow.
- Small half eggshells can be made into boats or nests.

Day of the Dead

Europeans aren't the only ethnic crafters who use sugar in sculpture. The people of Mexico make little sugar skulls for Dia de los Muertos, or "Day of the Dead," a centuries-old celebration in which the departed are honored and remembered by the living with joyous celebration every November 2.

1 1/2 hours

MARBLEIZED PAPER

Marbleized paper was invented at least 700 years ago by the people of Turkey, who used the unique paper as a way to keep people from forging official Turkish documents. Making marbleized paper can be a little messy, so you may want to work outdoors.

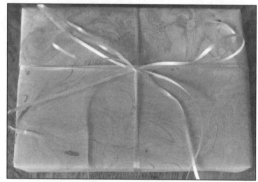

WHAT YOU NEED

- Paper cups and stirrers (Popsicle sticks and twigs work well)
- Food coloring (for Easy Method)
- Cooking oil (for Easy Method)
- Jar (for Advanced Method)
- Acrylic or fabric paint (for Advanced Method)
- Water thickener such as liquid starch or powdered laundry starch, carrageenan, or gum tragacanth (available from art supply stores) (for Advanced Method)

Easy-Method Preparation

Fill several small paper cups about 1/3 full of cooking oil. Drop different colors of food coloring into each one and stir them thoroughly with a stick.

- Flat tray such as a flat cardboard box lined with plastic, aluminum roasting pan, or clean cat litter pan (lined with plastic for easy cleanup)
- Small eyedroppers or squeeze bottles (available in pharmacies or left over from fabric paints)
- Pencils, straw brushes, or plastic forks
- Rubber gloves
- Old T-shirt or smock
- White paper or envelopes

❶ Fill the tray with water, liquid starch, or special thickened water until about 1" (2.5 cm) deep. With eyedroppers, add a few drops of your color into the water.

❷ Swirl the colors gently with a pencil, fork, or straw brush. Don't stir in the color — you want it to stay on the surface. (See page 143 for challenging design possibilities.)

❸ When you like the design, gently place your paper so it lies on top of the water without air bubbles under it.

Advanced-Method Preparation

One day before starting the project, stir the powdered water thickener into a large jar of water. It should have directions telling you how much to add, but if not, just add about ¼ cup (50 ml). Shake the jar to help the powder dissolve.

The next day, fill several small paper cups about ⅓ full of water. Squeeze in globs of acrylic paint and stir. Add enough paint to make it the consistency of thick cream.

4 Lift the paper off immediately and let it drip for a minute.

5 Hang the paper on a clothesline or drying rack, or place on a flat surface.

6 Gently stir the surface of the paint in the tray, or add new colors and swirl them. Pick up the new pattern with a new piece of paper.

7 Keep trying new colors and new combinations. Don't worry about making any mistakes. Each design is interesting and beautiful.

Challenging Designs

Use a pencil or a pin to make these swirls.

Bull's-eye. Drop colors one on top of another.

Heart. Drag a pencil or pin down the center of the bull's-eye.

Feathers. Add the colors, combing them lengthwise in one direction and then the other. Then, comb widthwise in one direction and then the other.

Star. Drag the pencil or pin away from the center of the heart to the edges.

Stone. Make splatters by loading a paintbrush with a color and tapping it above the pan.

Freeform. Just swirl the colors until you like the way the design looks.

Drop colors

Comb right

Comb down

Feather

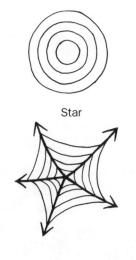

Heart

Star

Marbleized Covers

If you have any really old books (such as dictionaries) around your house, check to see if they have marbleized paper inside the front and back covers. Originally books were bound in leather, but later, people started using less expensive materials and covering them with beautiful marbleized paper.

LANDSCAPE CAKE

Level of challenge: 3

3 to 4 hours

WHAT YOU NEED

- Cake batter (homemade or from cake mix)
- Icing (see page 147)
- Candies (see ideas on page 148)

E*at a mountain or a computer! Create a volcano for dessert, or a lake with alligators that you eat! Use your imagination to create a yummy cake of your favorite place or thing on earth.*

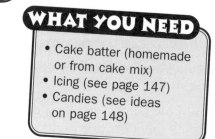

Basic Cake Landscape Base

To make a big cake for a whole party of kids, make at least 6 times a normal-size cake recipe. Use any flour cake recipes or cake mixes you like. The cake is just the raw material for creating the scene. Certain cake flavors are good for certain landscapes: Chocolate cake makes great mountains and volcanoes, strawberry and cherry cakes are good for southwestern scenes, and yellow cake with raspberry jam added looks like granite!

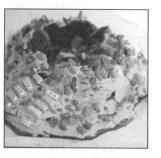

Setting the Scene

Have you ever seen a topographical map? Each line on the map indicates a change in elevation. On the map, a mountain will look like a bull's-eye of concentric circles, but if you were there and wanted to get to the center of the circle, you would be hiking uphill!

Layered Mountains

❶ Pour some cake batter into several cookie sheets (with sides) and, with grown-up help, bake according to package or recipe directions, checking often to avoid burning.

❷ Cut a large piece of cake for the bottom layer or base of the mountain; then, cut each successive layer smaller so they gradually look like the concentric circles of a topographical map or stack like a pile of large-to-small pancakes.

❸ Stack the cakes with layers of icing between them (see icing recipes on page 147).

❹ Cover the cakes with icing to smooth the sides.

Elevated Landscape

Round Cake Mountains

❶ Pour batter into angel food cake pans and, with grown-up help, bake according to package or recipe directions.

❷ Use the whole cake as a mountain, or cut the cake in half to make tall cliffs. Fill the indentations from the center tube for blue icing waterfalls.

❸ Pour cake batter into well-greased tin cans filled half full and bake. Different can sizes add variety, but don't try to use very narrow cans, because the cake won't come out easily. Use the cake shapes for mountains or towers.

Oceans and Watery Scenes

1 To make a lake or ocean, use blue icing or blue gelatin. Make the gelatin on a large, flat cookie sheet (with sides) or other large pan.

2 When the gelatin hardens, transfer sections of it to the cake with a spatula.

3 Make a smaller pond or a pool in the mountains by making gelatin in a clear bowl and then surrounding it with cake. Then, add the gelatin to the cake at the last minute.

Note: Do not use gelatin on a cake that will be served outside, because it will run and ruin the cake.

Putting It All Together

1 Decide what you want your landscape to look like; then, set up a large surface for the cake, such as a tabletop, a large piece of plywood, or strong cardboard. Cover the surface with a clean cloth or paper.

2 Lay out your cake in the design you've chosen, using icing wherever you will be putting candies and to smooth out the landscape. (In some places you may want to skip the icing if you want the color of the cake to show.)

MAKING COOL CRAFTS & AWESOME ART

3 Create a miniature world using various miniature candies. Set up little scenes in your big scene, such as a candy table, a candy umbrella, and a gummy bear selling hot dogs. You may want to put gummy bears in a boat or on a beach towel, or build houses out of caramel "bricks" and graham cracker "walls." (See page 148 for more ideas.)

4 Invite your friends over to eat. They will be glad to celebrate your creativity!

Basic Icing

This icing holds the cake layers together and makes a good foundation for decorations.

1 pkg. (8 oz) cream cheese
2 cups (500 ml) confectioners' sugar
1 teaspoon (5 ml) vanilla extract
Food coloring (optional)

Mix all ingredients together until creamy and smooth.

WHAT YOU NEED

- 4 T (50 ml) powdered egg white mixed with 1/2 cup (125 ml) water
- 2 cups (500 ml) sugar
- 1/2 teaspoon (2 ml) cream of tartar
- Vanilla or cocoa powder *(optional)*
- Food coloring *(optional)*

Amazing Microwave Icing

1 Stir together the sugar, cream of tartar, and 1 cup (250 ml) water in a microwave-safe glass measuring cup or bowl. Microwave for 3 to 5 minutes, until the mixture boils.

2 Ask a grown-up to help you beat the egg white mixture until it forms soft peaks (when the egg whites hold their shape but are not dry and stiff).

3 Ask a grown-up to help you hold the measuring cup with a hot pad and pour the hot mixture slowly on the beaten egg whites while beating at medium speed. Then beat the mixture for several minutes at high speed.

4 Add any flavorings and colorings you like. This will make a huge amount of fluffy, moldable frosting that will cover anything!

Plan Your Landscape

Local. Your house, your neighborhood, a park, a local farmers' market

Trips. Grand Canyon, a favorite lake or ocean, your summer camp

Maps. The world, the United States, Canada, your state

Imaginary. An imaginary world from a book, movie, or song

Favorite objects or pets. Computer, teddy bear, your St. Bernard!

Historical. Native village, Pompeii, ancient Egypt

Candy Characters and Treat Streets

- Gummy bear "folks"
- Chocolate cars and buses
- Good 'n' Plenty® "hot dogs"
- Rock candy on a stick "streetlights"
- Spearmint leaf "trees"
- Thin, black licorice rope "railroad tracks"
- Jelly bean "rocks, cobblestones, paths, eggs"
- Caramel square "bricks"
- Shredded coconut (dyed with food coloring) "grass, water, dirt, or snow"
- Graham cracker "walls" and "roofs"
- Tootsie Rolls® may be shaped into almost anything (warm them for about 20 seconds in the microwave)

PLAYABLE SCULPTURES

*M*ake a board with obstacles and goals for a marble to be propelled around. Once you've made a Playable Sculpture, you will see things in a new light. When your friend opens a birthday present, you'll be thinking what a wonderful marble machine the plastic packaging would make!

Bagatelle Pinball Machine

*P*inball is actually a kind of bagatelle, a popular game once played by wealthy people in France during the 1800s. The word *bagatelle* is also used in sayings. For instance, if someone says to you, "don't worry about that homework assignment, it's just a bagatelle," they probably mean that it's a small, unimportant thing.

It's Just a Bagatelle

WHAT YOU DO

❶ To make the rim, carefully hammer the nails around the edge of the board every inch (2.5 cm) or so.

❷ Make a bouncy fence by wrapping rubber bands around several nails at a time, all the way around the board. Overlap the bands a little.

❸ For starting the marble off, you need a shooter. You can use 2 nails and a thick rubber band that you pull back so that it shoots out the rubber band like a slingshot.

❹ Set up an obstacle course by gluing down objects for the marble to go around and through. You might use nails and rubber band fences, springs, corks, erasers, or pieces of wood.

⑤ To set up some noisemakers, carefully hammer 2 nails far enough apart so a rubber band can be stretched between them. Then, hang small bells from the rubber band, leaving just enough space for the marble to go under or through and jiggle the bells. Or, carefully nail a hole in 5 metal bottle caps and then stack them on a thin nail that you hammer into the wood. The caps will make a great sound when hit.

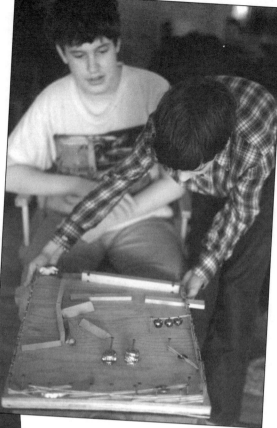

⑥ To make a paddle for hitting the marble back up into the play area, use a wood piece that is long and narrow (you could even use a pencil). Put it near the bottom of the board with a short end sticking outside the rubber band fence for you to grab. Make sure the paddle end has space to maneuver so that it can be used to hit the marble back up into the play area.

⑦ Prop up your board so that the far end is slightly higher than the end with the shooter and paddles.

⑧ Try out your pinball machine. You may want to decide on a scoring system and have fun challenging yourself with it.

Marble Machine

Y ou can use lots of stuff you have around that would usually get thrown away to make this fun toy. You will be making a path for the marble to roll down. The challenge is to make it complicated and interesting, but smooth enough so that the marble will not get caught or fall off on the way.

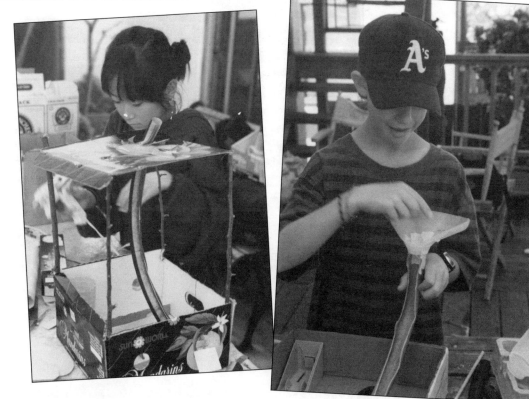

WHAT YOU NEED

- Cardboard box
- Large Styrofoam™ packing pieces
- Reusable items you've collected (see That's Recyclable! on page 153)
- Masking tape
- Marbles
- White craft glue or warm glue gun (ask a grown-up to help you set up a safe place for using this tool)

WHAT YOU DO

1 Choose a box and/or big Styrofoam™ packing piece and try to see what kind of path could be made on it. You can glue or tape on pieces of cardboard and plastic packaging to help form the path.

2 Make the path more complicated by gluing down recycled items for drop-offs, bridges, tunnels, and traps for the marble to go through. A section of bicycle tire can be used to make a path, or a section of old garden hose can be used as a tunnel. Let all glued areas dry completely.

Old-Time Marble Machines

Marble machines have been popular toys in America for years. Some of the old ones are made entirely of wood and have drop-offs that tilt and wheels that turn with the weight of the marble. Some huge marble machines have long, complicated paths and motors to bring the marble back up to the top to start again. Maybe your local museum has one!

3 Start a marble out at the top of your machine and see if it can successfully make it all the way through the path you have made. You'll probably have to make some changes before trying it again.

Terrific Trophies

You'll probably get really good at your pinball and marble machines, so you deserve a trophy! You can make them out of all kinds of old packaging that might normally get thrown away. Trophies are also a nice thing to make for someone you appreciate. Here's an idea:

1 Cut a plastic bottle about 3" (8 cm) from the top (puncture the plastic with scissors and cut around). The top part,

covered with aluminum foil and turned over, looks like a trophy cup. Decorate it with "jewels" made of crinkled-up candy wrappers and beads. Styrofoam™ curlicues look fancy on trophies, too.

2 The trophy cup can be glued onto a foil-covered plastic cottage cheese container. Remember, trophies are supposed to be gaudy, huge, and a little ridiculous!

That's Recyclable!

Look all around for interesting things to use in *Playable Sculptures*.

For Marble and Bagatelle Pinball Machines.

Almost anything that can be glued down to form a path or maze.

Pushpins, paper clips, straight pins
Miscellaneous cardboard pieces
Popsicle sticks
Bottle lids, all sizes (metal and plastic)
Springs from old spiral notebooks
Miscellaneous wood scraps, especially
   with curved sides
Old binders from office, school, or
   photo albums
Rubber bands
Bells
Keys
Rubber erasers
Corks
Thread spools
Metal washers
Plastic spoons
Metal cutting edge from waxed paper
   container

For Marble Machines Only.

Old hoses and bicycle tires (cut around
   the rim to remove the metal part;
   then, cut into sections)
Bicycle inner tubes, cut into sections
Plastic packaging with paths or holes
Styrofoam™ packaging with depressions,
   paths, and openings
Toilet paper tubes, paper towel tubes,
   wrapping paper tubes
Small plastic bottles (cut both ends to
   form tubes or cut one end to form a
   catch basin)
Shoe boxes, tissue boxes, cereal
   boxes, milk cartons

BORING STUFF FOR GROWN-UPS

ROUND · **ROUND**

Haste Thee Nymph

G major
2-3 parts
Circa 1700s

1 Haste thee ny-mph and bring wi-th thee Jest and___ yo-uth-ful___ jol-li-ty,
Do Do Ti La La Re Re Do Ti Mi Mi Re Do Re Mi Fa So So Do

2 Quips and__cranks and wan-ton__ wiles, Nods and__ becks and wreath-ed smiles,
Mi Mi Re Do Do Fa Fa Mi Re So So Fa Mi Re Do Do Re Mi

3 Spo-rt th-at wrink-led ca-re de-__rides and Laugh-ter___ hol-___ ding both his sides.
So Fa Mi Fa Do Mi Re Do Ti Do La Ti Do Do Re Mi Fa So So So So

Yes! Grown-Ups May Participate

I hope grown-ups will be so captivated by these projects they'll say, "Pass the scissors, I'm making one too!" When you join kids in doing these activities, you give them a chance to see grown-ups who like to have fun and try new things.

For most of the projects, there should be time for the grown-ups to enjoy crafting with the kids, too. If you like the craft project, any difficulties figuring out how to do it will be much easier to solve. When kids ask you questions, you don't have to know all the answers. You can wonder with them and work together to find the solutions!

Kids want to dive in; they're excited and full of ideas. Give encouragement and enjoy what they do. Help to set up the envi-

ronment so it is safe (see Safety First on page 12) and help keep it positive with lots of encouragement. Be available to help solve design problems or to add an extra pair of hands when needed. But avoid directing the projects too much or defining how they should be done. Instead, let kids find their way with some minor direction from you. Allow them to learn from their mistakes and reinvent things. When kids ask for help, give them only the help they need at the moment, and then let them go at it again. They'll remember what they learned better this way.

After supplying the tools and providing the safe setting, give kids the space to experiment. They'll problem-solve on their own and help each other. Don't rush in with solutions too fast. And remember to encourage individual creativity. No project has to be "right" or perfect. Approach the time together with openness and patience. Kids will ask for help, advice, and wisdom when they are ready. Then, you can be there.

Fun. Kids will have fun doing these projects. Real education is joyful, a celebration of creative thought. Each child has a claim to fame. These projects help them find their unique contribution to the world.

Mastery and self-esteem. These activities give children a sense of mastery. If we try a lot of new things with kids, they can learn that they don't have to be experts to do things they've never done before, and they don't need an "expert" to do it for them. It gives them a sense of widening possibilities rather than feeling restricted and fearful in our modern world.

Control. If kids are given more control over their lives and surroundings, they will contribute more and take better care of their environment.

Variety. Kids get a chance to use a lot of unusual materials in unique ways. Children are naturally inventive, and a variety of materials encourages individualized thought.

Beauty. Much of what kids create is beautiful — not perfect, but beautiful in its idiosyncracies.

What These Experiences Offer Kids

Active observation. Kids learn to actively observe our world. By being involved in doing, kids become more alert and observe more closely. Because they are not being "taught at," but instead are "discovering with," they become their most intelligent selves.

Integrated curriculum. Kids learn how every bit of learning ties to other bits of learning. From each activity, they can branch out into many intellectual disciplines if they so choose.

Save the earth. We make things out of what we find so we can see where things come from and how they recycle themselves. By being frugal without being miserly, kids get maximum enjoyment out of minimal materials. The discovery of new applications is exciting in its own right.

Culture. Kids will draw on a variety of cultural roots, enjoying the "old ways" and valuing our different histories. Respect for others is a natural outgrowth of the shared experience of making art.

Enjoy unpredictable exuberance! As you work with kids, try to let go of control and allow wildness. It's really more fun. Let your house be lived in, share your garden with animals. That doesn't mean you should abandon all house cleaning and ignore the garden, but allow for creative messes indoors and natural processes outdoors. Your kids will appreciate it!

INDEX

MORE GOOD BOOKS FROM WILLIAMSON PUBLISHING

Kids Can!® Books

The following *Kids Can!*® books for ages 4 to 10 are each 160-178 pages, fully illustrated, trade paper, 11 x 8 ¹/₂, $12.95 US.

HAND-PRINT ANIMAL ART ($14.95; full color)
by Carolyn Carreiro

CUT-PAPER PLAY!
Dazzling Creations from Construction Paper
by Sandi Henry

Early Childhood News Directors' Choice Award
VROOM! VROOM!
Making 'dozers, 'copters, trucks & more
by Judy Press

Children's BOMC Main Selection
BOREDOM BUSTERS! (Newly Revised)
The Curious Kids' Activity Book
by Avery Hart and Paul Mantell

Benjamin Franklin Best Juvenile Nonfiction Award
American Bookseller Pick of the Lists
SUPER SCIENCE CONCOCTIONS
50 Mysterious Mixtures for Fabulous Fun
by Jill Frankel Hauser

Parents' Choice Gold Award
Parents Magazine Parents' Pick
THE KIDS' NATURE BOOK (Newly Revised)
365 Indoor/Outdoor Activities & Experiences
by Susan Milord

Benjamin Franklin Best Multicultural Book Award
Parents' Choice Approved
Skipping Stones Multicultural Honor Award
THE KIDS' MULTICULTURAL COOKBOOK
Food & Fun Around the World
by Deanna F. Cook

KIDS' COMPUTER CREATIONS
Using Your Computer for Art & Craft Fun
by Carol Sabbeth

Parents' Choice Approved
Dr. Toy Vacation Favorites Award
KIDS GARDEN!
The Anytime, Anyplace Guide to Sowing & Growing Fun
by Avery Hart and Paul Mantell

Oppenheim Toy Portfolio Best Book Award
American Bookseller Pick of the Lists
THE KIDS' SCIENCE BOOK
Creative Experiences for Hands-On Fun
by Robert Hirschfeld and Nancy White

Parents' Choice Gold Award
American Bookseller Pick of the Lists
Oppenheim Toy Portfolio Best Book Award
THE KIDS' MULTICULTURAL ART BOOK
Art & Craft Experiences from Around the World
by Alexandra M. Terzian

Little Hands® Books

The following *Little Hands®* books for ages 2 to 6 are each 144 pages, fully illustrated, trade paper, 10 x 8, $12.95 US.

Other Books from Williamson Publishing

American Bookseller Pick of the Lists

PYRAMIDS!
50 Hands-On Activities to Experience Ancient Egypt
   by Avery Hart and Paul Mantell
   96 pages, 10 x 10
   Trade paper, $12.95

Benjamin Franklin Best Juvenile Fiction Award
Parents' Choice Honor Award
Skipping Stones Multicultural Honor Award

TALES ALIVE!
Ten Multicultural Folktales with Activities
   by Susan Milord
   128 pages, 8 1/2 x 11
   Trade paper, $15.95

Benjamin Franklin Best Juvenile Fiction Award
Parents' Choice Approved
Benjamin Franklin Best Multicultural Book Award

TALES OF THE SHIMMERING SKY
Ten Global Folktales with Activities
   by Susan Milord
   128 pages, 8 1/2 x 11
   Trade paper, $15.95

To see what's new at Williamson and learn more about specific books, visit our website at:

http://www.williamsonbooks.com

To Order Books:

You'll find Williamson books at your favorite bookstore or order directly from Williamson Publishing. We accept Visa and MasterCard (please include the number and expiration date), or send check to:

Williamson Publishing Company
Church Hill Road, P.O. Box 185
Charlotte, Vermont 05445

Toll-free phone orders with credit cards:
1-800-234-8791

E-mail orders with credit cards:
order@williamsonbooks.com

Catalog request:
   mail, phone, or e-mail

Please add **$3.00** for postage for one book plus **50 cents** for each additional book. Satisfaction is guaranteed or full refund without questions or quibbles.

Prices may be slightly higher when purchased in Canada.

Kids Can!®, *Little Hands*®, and *Tales Alive!*® are registered trademarks of Williamson Publishing.
Kaleidoscope Kids™ is a trademark of Williamson Publishing.